Inside The WILD

L.W. Oakley

Oakley

Published by

 **GENERAL STORE PUBLISHING HOUSE**

499 O'Brien Rd., Box 415, Renfrew, Ontario, Canada K7V 4A6
Telephone (613) 432-7697 or 1-800-465-6072
www.gsph.com

ISBN: 978-1-897113-52-3
Printed and bound in Canada

Cover design, formatting and printing by
Custom Printers of Renfrew Ltd.

Library and Archives Canada Cataloguing in Publication

Oakley, Larry, 1954-
    Inside the wild / Larry Oakley.

Short stories:

ISBN-13: 978-1-897113-52-3

    I. Title.

PS8629.A55I68 2007   C813'.6   C2006-905025-2

For Abbey

CONTENTS

Acknowledgement

Preface

Book One—Hunting
1. 'Twas the night before opening day . . .
2. The old camp
3. First time (part 1)
4. First time (part 2)
5. "We will all take a turn in the swamp"
6. The fate of Thunder
7. There was a wolf inside him
8. To be successful at killing
9. "Daddy, how can you kill Bambi?"
10. Sparing life
11. It happened because he wanted to hunt
12. The essence of hunting
13. The moment a wild animal becomes meat
14. The camp cook and the great composer
15. Wildlife transformed into art
16. "I've done enough killing"
17. Blood, bullets and words
18. Hunt Club in a hundred-acre wood
19. The bedtime story

Book Two—Wildlife
1. "Wee, sleekit, cow'rin, tim'rous beastie"
2. This is not a fairy tale
3. Battle for survival
4. It looks like freedom and feels like sex
5. Richard the rooster
6. De-beaked chicken soup

7. Bullheadin' in Shakespeare's "undiscovered country"

8. Turkey vultures ride on nature's gravy train

9. Death the Impaler

10. Feeding wild animals for your own pleasure

11. "He who sits in the shadow of his tail"

12. Watching wild animals

Book Three—The Wilderness

1. We have a place

2. Worlds of discovery

3. The symphony

4. Queen of night

5. The causeway fishin' hole

6. The spirit in the woods

7. The greater sin

8. *"C'est la cuisine sauvage"*

9. Call of the wild

10. Most powerful symbol of wilderness

11. What happens when the wilderness responds

12. I am a place that you may never know

ACKNOWLEDGEMENT

I would like to thank Steve Lukits, Ph.D., head of the English Department at the Royal Military College of Canada in Kingston, Ontario.

During his time as editor of *The Kingston Whig-Standard*, he published my work and helped me become a writer. After publishing my first piece, he gave me a copy of *The Bear*, by William Faulkner. I was never the same person after reading it.

Without Steve Lukits, I would not have written this book.

PREFACE

Delivering the meat was my first job as a boy. I was fourteen when I began working part-time at a butcher shop.

Every Saturday, I helped one of the owners make deliveries in a white van loaded with cardboard boxes filled with groceries and meat. We drove from our side of Toronto's Don Valley River into Rosedale, which is one of the richest neighbourhoods in Canada. Jimmie did the driving and I carried the boxes from the van into the houses.

Most houses in Rosedale were more like mansions. Many had small signs that said, "Make deliveries at the back door."

Those houses and signs were an important part of my early education. The people living there had money and my family didn't. Because of that job at the butcher shop, I paid attention in school and never had to be told to do my homework. I knew at an early age that I would get a good education and have money. For me, school was never fun. It was necessary.

When I rang the bell at the back door or side entrance, the owner never answered. It was always a maid or a cook. "There's someone like me," I would think to myself.

I carried the boxes into big shiny kitchens with walk-in coolers like the one at the butcher shop. Many of those kitchens were bigger than the butcher shop and some of the houses in my neighbourhood.

There was a long wooden table and bench built into the wall in the back of the butcher shop where the butchers sat and drank rye and water and studied racing forms. A bookmaker came by every Friday night to take bets on horses. He had a bigger car than everyone in our neighbourhood and always seemed happy. He came back on Saturday to collect his money, but he didn't act too happy then.

The bookie contributed to my education too. He gave me some good advice once. He asked, "Do you want a good tip on the races?"

Before I could answer he laughed and said, "*Don't* bet on the horses."

Years later, after I moved to Kingston and became an accountant, I started carrying meat in my knapsack on Saturday mornings. This time I carried it into the woods during our weekly hikes. This meat came from animals that I had killed myself. It wasn't beef or chicken. It was venison and moose. We would stop in the woods and build a small hearth with rocks and cook the wild meat over a wood fire. I told my friends at the fire about my boyhood job, and someone said, "You're still delivering the meat."

Now I get to deliver the meat in a third way. Maybe the best way of all.

I could have left Kingston many times. Once I was offered a promotion and transfer back to Toronto to a job with an important title and big office at the corner of King and Bay streets, the heart of corporate Canada. But I decided not to go.

I was a member of a hunting camp and had learned not just to hunt, but about the wilderness and the animals living there. I didn't want to give that up. I wanted to stay close to it.

Eventually I started writing stories about the outdoors, nature, and hunting in *The Kingston Whig-Standard*. I always mailed my mother and father a copy of the newspaper whenever I was published. It was one of the ways I spoke to them—through my stories.

When I decided to stay in Kingston I didn't know I had Indian blood. I didn't know that my great-grandmother, Rose Anna Monette, was a Mohawk woman from Oka. That makes me an octoroon or one-eighth Indian. I'm now a member of the Ontario Metis Aboriginal Association.

I believe now that my great-grandmother's spirit spoke to me about hunting and the woods when it was time to decide whether to go back to the big city. One day, after reading one of my hunting stories, my mother told me that she felt like she was there with me in the woods, and that she had been to those places before.

"Why do you say that?" I asked.

"Because my grandmother was an Indian and we all share the same blood," she answered.

Now I have written a book about hunting, wild animals, and the wilderness. But the book is really about life.

I'm no longer delivering the meat from a butcher shop or only in the backwoods. I'm delivering the meat in the pages of this book. The words are the meat. This time I'm delivering my own meat—the meat that is my life.

The meat of this book is given to nourish the spirit in the same way my spirit received nourishment inside the wild.

BOOK ONE
HUNTING

CHAPTER 1

There was a hunter in our camp who was quiet when he was sober but acted crazy when he was drunk, like some men do whether they hunt or not. Once, he took his shotgun down from the wall and blew one of the windows out while everyone was sitting around the camp playing cards. I can't remember why he did that and doubt he could either.

When he got really drunk, he sometimes said he was going to kill us all and then kill himself. He said he was going to shoot us while we were in bed sleeping. He said it more than once, too, and some of the men were worried, including me.

We talked about him when he wasn't around or after he passed out drunk on his bunk. One night during deer hunting he talked about it again.

I told him: "Eddie, when you decide it's time to kill everyone and commit suicide, why don't you spare me? I'll tell your story. I'll say it wasn't your fault. I'll say they drove you to it. I'll say they had it coming."

In front of everyone—and we were all there—Eddie replied, "I like that. Consider yourself saved."

'Twas the night before opening day . . .

People wait all year for Christmas. But hunters count the months, weeks, and days to another day, the first Monday in November—opening day of deer hunting season in Ontario.

The evening before opening day is like the night before Christmas to men who return to the camps and re-enter the woods for two short-lived but long-awaited weeks.

Dinner on the eve of opening day is the first of many rituals at our hunting camp, which is called The Terrible Ten. We hunt on a couple of hundred acres in the Third Lake–Loon Lake area between Verona and Enterprise in southeastern Ontario. Like the traditional Christmas feast in many homes, turkey is often prepared, usually stuffed, and sometimes served with dumplings. The turkey we eat on Sunday night is one received the previous Christmas from the employer of a camp member who saves it in his freezer for eleven months. Other meals are basically the same as they have been for years: steak on Monday, baked ham on Tuesday, and fresh deer heart and liver on Wednesday or Thursday. Leftover turkey will be eaten later in sandwiches on the "watches," where the hunters wait for deer to pass by so they can try to kill them.

A large wooden table surrounded by chairs is in the centre of every hunting camp, just as the kitchen is at the centre of the home. After the supper dishes are cleared, washed, dried, and put away, and after the dogs are fed and the fire stoked, round baking tins filled with homemade cookies and cupcakes are put out.

Some hunters eat their sweets with tea or coffee. But wherever there is a hunting camp table, there is a bottle on it. Like other bottles on other tables, some people drink from it and others don't. Of those who drink, some drink more and some drink less.

Many hunters who drink, sit and drink continuously. I have watched them. Like great snakes devouring their own tails, they are slowly devoured by the contents of the bottles they drink from. Every camp, like most families, has at least one drunk and, like most drunks, they know who and what they are.

Talk runs high on the eve of opening day. Topographic maps are removed from cardboard cylinders and spread across the table. As the runs are planned and the watches taken for the next day, fingers point at places on a map. "That's where we lifted that deer last year," someone says. Or, "That's where it disappeared." But the places they point to are just open spaces on the map that don't have names printed beside them like the small black dots that do.

The names of these places have never been printed on a map or recorded in a book or written down on a piece of paper, but that doesn't mean they are nameless. They are called "the double dams" or "the mash" or "the Congo," names that are well known to the men around the table. They named the places where deer are often killed and where hunters wait on their watches while eating their leftover turkey sandwiches.

As they stare at the map, they remember seeing a deer or watching it disappear or shooting it. For an instant they are caught up in the memory of that past moment and fall silent. If you've been in a hunting camp and sat at that table and stared at the map and watched those fingers point and heard those words spoken, you will remember how it was when the deer was right there, in the woods, because you're suddenly there, too.

Spellbound, you are transported to that unmarked place on the map. It's a place you once had to be taken to and shown by someone who told you where to stand, which way to look, and how to be ready; and, most important, not to leave until a hunter came back and got you, even on those days when you arrived there before the sun came up and left after it went down.

It's a place that you eventually had to find the hard way, on your own, but only after you said you could. It's a place that you finally found without getting lost or turned around. It's a place where a deer tried to

Author wearing orange coat and holding rifle at a typical unmarked place on the map where hunters wait and watch.

sneak past one morning when you were waiting beneath the crest of a ridge where you were told to wait while looking towards a clump of cedars where you were told to look.

It's a place that you will never forget, because one day, after you left it, you started calling yourself a hunter.

By the time everyone goes to bed, it's usually well after midnight. Like children, hunters usually sleep in bunks and in one room. Most hunters are grown men who snore and talk in their sleep. On the night before opening day, they dream about deer and a lone buck (it's always a buck, and a big one) standing unaware or walking toward you without fear—if it hasn't seen you shake or heard you twitch or smelled the panic in your sweat. If it does sense you, then you see it over your gun—not like meat on the hoof, but still alive, running and bounding away before being killed and stretched out dead hanging from the branch of a tree.

The hunting camp has rites older than Christmas, as old as the first cave dwelling and the hunters who gathered there. The camp is a place where men withdraw to and feel safe in. Late at night, it's a place where men bare their souls and tell the truth about their lives to other men, especially the mistakes they regret and the feelings they keep hidden and seldom admit to having.

I have heard them. And I have taken my turn: not as a sinner does, confessing to a priest before being given penance to do, or as a prisoner addressing a jury of his peers before sentence is passed, but like a prodigal son, returning home, expecting and receiving nothing, not even forgiveness.

When the alarm rings at 4:30 a.m., everyone gets up immediately, including the drunks. And it's just like waking up on Christmas morning and being a little boy again.

But it's not that kind of morning for the deer. The older, smarter ones know what day it is because it comes around every year, along with the rut and the colder, shorter days. The young deer fawns born that spring don't know about opening day. Their mothers can't tell them what to expect the way our mothers told us what happens on December 25.

Fawns find out about opening day the hard way, by surprise, the same way all those turkeys discover that Christmas is a day so special that most people wait all year for it.

CHAPTER 2

Two hours before daylight, we were eating breakfast in our canvas army tent. When someone put ketchup on his omelet, the man who cooked it pointed at the omelet and said, "In an expensive restaurant, that would be an insult to the chef."

A short time later, our chef said to me, "I fell asleep last night while you were telling that story about Shackleton. What happened after they became stranded on that island in Antarctica?"

"It's also an insult to fall asleep when I'm telling a story," I replied. "I don't repeat my bedtime stories. I only tell them at night when everyone is in bed and the lights are out."

People laugh when they hear that bedtime stories have become one of the rituals of our annual moose hunting trip. I deer hunt with a different gang. They laughed too. But last year I started telling bedtime stories to them.

Hunters were the first storytellers and the first artists. They told their stories and made their paintings in caves, places that once knew only silence and darkness. Some of their paintings are still on the walls of those caves. Those first paintings also tell stories. People are rarely depicted. Instead, images of mammoths and bison herds and wounded boar tell us that ancient man was in awe of the power and speed and spirit of the animals he hunted and killed. Those feelings inspired primeval hunters with a wonder that made them the first storytellers. It happened during a time so long ago that it's called prehistory.

Our hunting camp had ten men. The members included fathers and sons, brothers, cousins, brothers-in-law, and friends. They had nicknames like Crow and Stuffer and Ace and Flint.

Like most hunting camps, ours had a name. It was called The Terrible Ten. The name was a warning. In cities and towns, we were at the mercy of people with education and money and social skills. At home, we were housebroken. But back at the camp and in the woods, we did what we wanted. There were men in that camp who would turn on you, or on each other. Eventually they turned on me.

Other gangs around us go by names such as Circle Game, The School House Gang and The Ponderosa. The deer we hunt move back and forth between their lands and ours.

Before I joined the camp, the men who started it scraped and pooled their money together to buy a couple hundred acres to use for hunting. The 125-year-old log farmhouse that came with the land needed to be patched and hammered into shape. That farmhouse became our camp, a place to gather and return to, a place to make a fire and

One of the Terrible Ten with a buck in the back of his pickup truck in front of the old camp.

keep the weather out, and a place to eat, sleep, and hang deer during hunting season. In time, it became like an old friend.

The "old camp," as we called it, had few amenities. It had one room downstairs and one upstairs.

The downstairs contained a home-built wood stove, a dirty looking fridge, two cookstoves, and three lights powered by propane gas. The kitchen area was at one end of the room, and the stairway and only door, inside or out, was at the other.

Suppertime inside the old camp.

Two long tables with an odd assortment of chairs made of chrome and vinyl or wood were in the centre. Someone from the camp carried one of those chairs into the woods to his watch to sit on while deer hunting. It's still out there. But no one has sat on it for years. It's rotting away and barely visible on the ground. We call that place the "chair watch."

We couldn't afford to buy furniture. So we hand-picked heavy old and torn couches from the dump and placed them along the walls of our camp. Our gun racks were above the couches and were filled with rifles and shotguns when we came there to hunt. Some men in the camp brought two or more. The first time I walked through the door and looked at the walls and saw those guns, I knew I was in a hunting camp.

Running water flowed into a rusted wash basin through a hose connected to two forty-five-gallon drums fastened to the outside wall and fed by the eavestrough. If there was no rain, we had no water.

Upstairs had ten bunks and makeshift dressers. You could see downstairs by looking through the spaces between the floorboards. A thick manila hemp rope tied to a beam near the only window was our fire escape. The rope came from a room at the old Tamworth Hotel where it was used for the same purpose. Since everyone at the camp smoked in bed, Fred, our camp cook, decided we needed a rope fire escape too. A single light bulb with a switch dangled below the centre beam. It provided light so you could find your bunk at night and your clothes in the morning. One of the boys ran a wire from the light along the beam, down the stairs, and out the door to the battery of a truck.

We shared the camp with flies, mice, and birds. The outhouse was fifty yards from the door, just past the woodpile. If you had to have a shit at night you needed a flashlight. When you picked it up and headed out the door, there was always that little reminder from someone: "Be careful or a bear might get ya." My trips to the outhouse were always quick.

When deer season arrived, we would hunt all day and stay up all night drinking, talking, and playing cards. Fuelled by the energy of youth, we'd be out the door at first light, cheap baloney sandwiches in our pockets, old rubber boots on our feet, and hand-me-down guns over our shoulders. "Hurry up," someone would shout, "it's daylight in the swamp!"

Each year we told the same old stories: the first deer, the biggest deer, the longest shot. "Remember that big buck we got with the twisted rack?" or "Remember the time Red and Sam ran that deer all the way to Fourth Lake and back?" At the end of each hunting season, there were new tales to tell.

The camp had an old radio that was turned on in the morning to get the weather report and turned up in the evening to listen to country and western music. Everyone joined in when the radio played a Hank

Deer being hung on the meat pole outside the old camp.

Williams song. I remember singing along when Hank sang, "The silence of a falling star lights up a purple sky, and as I wonder where you are, I'm so lonesome I could cry." Whenever we drank and sang like that, we called it a "Hank Night."

As time passed, the old camp seemed colder, smaller, and less comfortable. It wasn't, of course. We had gotten older and more tired. We had become less terrible. We talked often about building a new camp. After a couple of years it happened. We beavered away at it every weekend from April through October. Friends, neighbours, and family members from the Verona area came to help until the last nail was driven home.

The new camp has plenty of creature comforts. There is electricity and plumbing. Other luxuries include a stereo, television, microwave, toilet, shower, and even a bathtub. All three bedrooms are carpeted. The new woodshed is almost the size of the old camp. The steel roof that we put on the old camp years ago to keep us dry was ripped off and nailed on our new woodshed to keep our firewood dry.

The Terrible Ten inside the new camp. I'm holding the rifle.

There are slippers by the wood stove and reading glasses on the night tables. When the day comes, some members of The Terrible Ten want their ashes spread around the camp. "And don't flush them down the toilet," they warn while pointing fingers and adding, "I mean it."

There are a lot of snapshots on the walls. Some show us building the new camp, sitting inside enjoying ourselves, and standing outside beside the meat pole with our deer. Many of the photos were taken in the woods and look the same. Men are posing with deer that they've just killed. A dead deer is sprawled out on the ground on its side with its white belly showing. A hunter wearing an orange coat and cap is crouching behind it. One hand is propping up the head by the antlers. The other hand is holding a rifle. There's a dark stain or smear across the thighs of his jeans where he wiped the blood from his hands after gutting the deer. He is unshaven and he is smiling.

Eventually, our attention returned to the old camp. "It's not safe," "It might fall down," "It's a fire hazard." We tried to sell it. We ran an ad in the newspaper for anyone interested in dismantling a 150-year-old log farmhouse. There were a couple of dozen calls, and about ten people went out to take a closer look, but there were no takers.

One April morning, we burned the old camp to the ground. Once the fire got going, the building just fell in on itself. It took hours to burn. There's a picture on the wall of the new camp that's framed and larger than all the rest. It's of the old camp. The barnboard nailed over the original logs of the farmhouse looks worn and grey. You can see how the walls are leaning and where the roof is sagging. The photo was taken minutes before the old camp collapsed while the fire blazed inside.

The old camp burning down.

Eventually we got tired of standing while it burned, so we sat on the ground and watched it go. Gary Knox remembered that his wife's grandmother used to ride by horse and buggy all the way out to this very house from Verona. "She came out to Saturday night hoedowns during the summer." In those days, Verona was still called Richardson.

As we sat, there were long periods of silence, broken every so often by just a few words:

"Hard to believe a family once lived here."

"I wonder how long it took them to build it."

"They must have cleared the land and grown their own food. They must have fished and hunted just to survive."

CHAPTER 3

If there are a lot of hunters in your gang or you're running deer in a small bush, sometimes you can see the hunter on the next watch. Two men can be as close as a hundred yards.

Wilf and I were about that distance apart the morning I saw him do something unusual on his watch. He was at one end of the beaver swamp and I was at the other.

A half-hour had passed and the dogs hadn't started yet when Wilf put down his gun. He collected pieces of wood from the ground and built a small fire, which isn't unusual. Hunters often build fires to keep warm, especially older men like Wilf.

But then Wilf started to undress. First he took off his orange hunting coat and pants. When he removed his boots I raised my rifle and began watching him through my scope making sure the safety was on and my finger was far away from the trigger.

I grinned to myself when he began unbuttoning his red full-length underwear, the kind with the button-down flap in the back. When he put them in the fire, I heard myself say, "Jesus," out loud. Then he got dressed again.

Later, I asked him what happened. He said, "I farted and shit myself."

FIRST TIME (PART 1)

Late the previous afternoon, Old Jimmie had found fresh tracks from the big buck crossing a dirt road and entering the patch of bush the men of the hunting camp called "the gauntlet." They had never actually seen the big buck. They knew him only from tracks that were bigger than any they had ever seen and from the scrapes he made on the ground and the rubs he left on trees to mark his territory.

Near dawn the next day, nine men surrounded the woods, waiting for the dogs to be brought forward so the hunt could begin. The wait before the hunt is a time of preparation and reflection. Hunters watch and listen intently to the world around them while each is alone with his thoughts.

Winnie stood overlooking a beaver dam where he had once killed a deer. It skidded and stumbled when it was hit, but was up standing again just as quickly. He remembered raising his gun a second time and seeing the deer lower its head while snorting blood from its nose. Then he could see himself standing over the deer and looking down at its open eyes and the dark red spots of spray on the forest floor.

No one else had shot a deer at the dam. They called it "Winnie's Watch." He liked that. He was alone there now, and no one could hear him if he spoke. He said "Winnie's Watch" out loud and smiled at the sound of his own words.

Young Jimmie, Old Jimmie's son, waited on a cedar ridge, admiring the beauty of his weapon. It was a classic Remington rifle, with a blued barrel and walnut stock. It felt solid and powerful and made him feel alive. He owned fifteen guns in all. He called them his "cannons," in the same manner an old woman might lovingly refer to her pet cats as "my babies."

Fred was near the edge of a swamp. He was the camp cook, so he didn't do dishes. He always left a mess because he knew someone else would clean it up. He was thinking: "Tonight I'll make a casserole with macaroni elbows, two cans of tomatoes, two cans of mushrooms, a chopped onion, and some hamburg."

"Somebody might complain," he said to himself. "I'll just tell them to cook the next meal if they don't like it." But no one ever complained. They didn't want to be the cook.

Fred, the camp cook, frying venison sausages and steaks on the grill at the new camp.

Slag was perfectly still and quiet. He used his foot to scrape away the dead leaves and twigs so he stood inside a circular patch of bare earth on the ground. If he needed to move his feet, even an inch or two, there would be no sound. "Don't move on your watch until you're ready to shoot, and when you move never make a sound," he always said.

Slag's brother, Steve, was on the watch near the dirt road where the deer had entered the bush. He had already smoked three cigarettes, lighting one with the other. He had smoked and drunk too much the night before. He remembered a time when, after a night like that, a cigarette the next day made him feel sick. But now he needed to smoke. It made him feel better.

Boney was on the next watch overlooking a creek that ran between two ridges. A lot of deer had been shot there over the years. They called it the "good watch," and when someone hadn't killed a deer for a long time this is where they came. They called him Boney because he had "a hungry look about him." He, too, had been up late. He was cold and tired and he sat down on a rock to try to get comfortable. He listened to the strange sounds of the forest and knew them all, just as he knew the sound of a deer. If one came, he would hear it before he saw it. His finger touched the safety on his gun. "Always be ready," he told himself.

Old Jimmie waited and watched, too. He wanted this buck. He didn't bother shooting the does or fawns any more, just bucks like the one tattooed beneath the shoulder of his right arm. He never told the others about how he hunted just for bucks now. "They might not understand." "But somehow," he thought to himself, "they already know."

Ronnie had started out early. He walked a long way in the dark to his watch. He knew the woods because he grew up in them. He didn't use a compass or need a watch when he hunted, although he had both.

His nephew, Ben, was only eighteen. It was his first time deer hunting and he had never seen a deer while holding a loaded gun in his hands, let alone the big buck they called "The Man." But he had heard the stories long before he entered the woods that day, and now the thought of seeing the big buck frightened him.

In the distant sky, he noticed a long, dark, waving ribbon of ducks. Seconds later, they passed overhead.

It was daylight in the swamp.

CHAPTER 4

Each camp has a killer. That's a hunter who likes to kill. His hunting trip is a success only if he kills something. He takes the best watches and hunts hard, even hunting alone after everyone has returned to the camp. He becomes jealous and gets upset whenever someone in his gang shoots a deer and he hasn't killed one yet.

In our camp the killer went by the nickname Pike Eyes, or Pike for short. His father hunted with us, too. Pike was guilty of the two cardinal sins of hunting: drinking on his watch and leaving garbage in the woods.

One afternoon he was hunting alone and watching a clover field until dark. He drank beer from a bottle while he watched. Before long, he needed to piss. So he pissed in the beer bottle and put the cap back on as tightly as he could. That way, the smell of urine wouldn't escape and be detected by a deer approaching from downwind.

He left the beer bottle lying on the ground at the watch.

The next morning, his father went out to hunt with the rest of us at first light. He took the watch his son was on the afternoon before.

After he had been there a while, he got thirsty. I remember when he told the story back at camp, how he said, "I thought to myself, what a break, someone left a beer at this watch, and it's cold, too, because it's been here all night."

So he drank. He only swallowed one mouthful. But that was enough for me.

The three biggest hounds, including the lead dog, Garth, were brought to the edge of the woods, tied tight in the back of a truck. They had only a few inches of slack, just enough to sit and stand, so an overly anxious hound wouldn't hang itself by jumping from a moving truck with a rope around its neck.

The dogs were released, and disappeared into the woods. A single dogger followed slowly behind. His footsteps crunched on the frost that covers the northern woods on November mornings.

Inside the woods, the scent from the deer hovered near the cold hard ground. The forest is a place of smell and sound, and the dogs searched for both.

An hour passed. Then everyone heard the dogs strike the scent as they began to howl in ecstasy. The big buck was browsing at a stand of young cedars. He raised his head immediately and turned one ear slightly back to the right to find the position and direction of the dogs. They were moving through the tall pines that filled the gap between two granite ridges where he had spent the previous night resting but not sleeping. The dogs had almost reached the long narrow swamp where the pines and ridges ended. The deer was at the far end of the swamp, looking and walking away from the sound of the dogs.

He doesn't understand why he's hunted any more than he understands a passing pickup truck. He only wants to survive.

He has never left his home inside the woods, nor will he.

He has no nest, no cave, and no hole to hide or take shelter in.

His mind is clear and quiet and free of doubt. He doesn't fear the hunters or the dogs. He knows them too well. If he fears anything at all, it's the men with axes and saws who cut him off from the forest one tree at a time.

When he finally began to run, he took the dogs around tag alder swamps, into swale holes, and through tangled undergrowth. When he ran hard, he left deep tracks behind. In some places, they appeared on the ground over twenty feet apart. These running leaps made his scent more difficult to follow and put distance between him and the dogs.

This gave him time to stop and look and listen for movement and search for strange smells that came from body soap, toothpaste, and burning cigarettes. He knew this meant danger was ahead. A big buck knows his world well. His nose receives messages from his only true friend and constant companion, the wind. His eyes can spot the slightest twitch, even at night, and his ears, which are the size of a man's open hand, will find you before his nose and eyes do.

The dogs had run him before, but, like the hunters, they had never seen him. Only the lead hound was still in the hunt, the hound with the big feet and big chest. He was still with the big buck when he circled the bush a second time, still invisible to the nine men who waited.

No man has ever seen him because he is an animal living at the edge, between darkness and light, partly in the open and partly concealed, able to hide in plain sight. He walks around open meadows and fields, not across them. He doesn't use the big channels and game trails taken by other animals. He follows a path made in his mind. He slips through creases, seams, and time.

The hunters had never seen him but knew he was there. They had no doubt that a living leg left those big tracks. When they knelt to touch them, they felt his weight and saw his size. He left calling cards for them but only on the thickest trees: a stripped patch of bark, higher up than it should be. These marks were made with his antlers and are a sign of his strength and a warning to other bucks. Everybody likes to be in awe of something, and the hunters in the woods that day were in awe of him. At night, in their camp, when they sat near their fires and talked, they called him a "monster."

The nine men on their watches continued waiting for him as he moved silently and secretly like some great fish through the deep. He has passed the watches where they waited a thousand times and will pass those places a thousand times more. But not if they are there. He does the watching then.

The buck had watched them wait before, knowing they would eventually leave as night fell. He learned how to be patient from standing outside, day and night, waiting for winters to end. They had even passed within feet of him as he crouched, hidden and motionless, the shadow of a shadow.

He knew many of the men individually from the sounds they made while striking matches and flicking lighters and eating food as they stood on their watches trying to be quiet.

This time there was one hunter he didn't know and he watched him now. It was the young boy, the first-time hunter. Usually, this watch was left open. The deer had used it before to slip through the gauntlet and outrun the dogs.

The boy was moving about, standing then crouching, trying to see and remain unseen. When the boy looked behind him, the deer knew he was afraid, just as he knew the dog was closing fast. It was then he picked the boy. The buck breathed deeply, gathering all his strength in one breath, and decided to run right at him.

He was thirty yards away when the boy heard the crash and saw him coming. The deer appeared like a ghost emerging from the green grey November woods, his legs and body bounding, his big rack rocking and tilting like the outstretched wings of some great bird in flight.

The boy's heart was beating rapidly as his world narrowed to the end of a pointed gun. But now the dog was there at the far end of his sight, running and reaching for the deer like a lion in chase grasping for its prey. The boy could not squeeze the trigger.

That night, around the table at the camp, they talked about the big buck, the lead dog and the first-time hunter. They spoke of the courage of the charge, and the determination of the chase, and the power of the shot that was never fired.

The deer was resting in some safe hideaway far away from the gauntlet and the dogs and guns.

The dog was waiting to be fed, chained to his rotting wooden doghouse just beyond the light from a window.

The boy never returned to the camp. A man sat listening in his place.

CHAPTER 5

It was done because the moose was killed late that day. There wasn't time to drag his body out of the woods. It was already dark when everyone arrived at the kill site to help.

He was gutted, and then the blood was drained from his open body cavity. This would attract wolves and bears. Something had to be done to keep them away until morning.

Someone spread an orange hunting coat across the moose. It was meant as a warning sign. Before returning to camp, the men formed a circle around the dead animal, taking care not to stand too close to each other or to the moose. Then everyone took a piss. That's what wild animals fear: the scent of man.

"WE WILL ALL TAKE A TURN IN THE SWAMP"

It was just a swamp. But the moment I saw it, I knew a big bull moose controlled it. A younger, less powerful and unproven bull couldn't hold such a place, especially during the rut, and the rut was on that morning when we arrived to call and hunt.

The swamp looked about a mile long. A hunter watching from one end would not see a full-grown moose walk out in the open across the other end. The swamp was wide and narrowed to about two hundred yards near its centre. That's where the beaver dam was. Right where it belonged.

The dam was big like everything else around the swamp, including the sky. One side held water covered with a thin coat of ice. The other side was filled with long wavy marsh hay that rippled in the wind like a field of ripening wheat. The swamp was surrounded by moss-covered granite ridges, clumps of cedar, and stands of pine. If you looked close and long, you would see that the landscape was cross-thatched by white birch trees with peeling strips of bark that exposed a layer of black beneath.

It was our fifth day of hunting up beyond the northern end of Lake Huron along the Spanish River near a place called McGregor Swamp. We hunted from a canvas army tent, with four eight-foot-long sections that were stitched and bound together over a frame of aluminum poles. Our table was an old door minus its hinges. There was a round hole in it where the doorknob once was. A pair of sawhorses served as legs. We slept on rusted army cots and used propane for cooking and lighting. Our floor was bare earth.

Every year, we camp on the same piece of ground. Over the years, it's become quite level because protruding rocks, exposed roots, and even small stumps, which were once inside our tent, have been removed.

We had set up our tent in the afternoon. As usual, it took more than two hours. It was a mild day and a clear sky when we began. But the

Army tent used as a moose-hunting camp. Cooking hearth is on the ground to the left; washtub and water jugs for drinking, cooking and washing are to the right.

weather in the north often changes suddenly. Within a half hour it was raining hard, but we kept going. It was too late to stop.

The last thing I do before leaving for moose hunting is the first thing I do when I return: I have a long, hot bath. While moose hunting, I never wash or brush my teeth. I try not to change my clothes. I enjoy being dirty not just for an hour or an afternoon but for the whole week. For me, it's an important part of the ritual. I give in to the dirt. I let my body be slowly encased by sweat and grime and grease. It makes me feel and smell and be more like the animals that I come to hunt.

At seven a.m. that morning, two miles from the tent, three of us lined up along one shoreline of the swamp. Francis was in the middle. As always, he did the calling. As the sun rose above the treeline behind us, the wind blew from our right to our left, down the full mile stretch of open swamp. My watch was downwind of Francis.

On the previous morning, Francis and I had scouted the opposite side of the swamp. At its edge there were flattened, oval-shaped patches in the marsh hay. They were moose beds. One was much larger than the others. It belonged to a big bull. But something important was missing from his bed, something that told us he wasn't far away. His was the only bed without frost in it.

The big bull that came to Francis's call that morning did not walk or charge out into the open directly toward the sound, the way a young eager-to-mate bull would. The big bull did something else. It was something you would expect from a wild animal that had managed to live so long and grow so big and become so wise in a place as harsh and unforgiving as the northern Ontario wilderness.

The moose is a shaggy, secret beast. A full-grown bull weighs about 1,500 pounds, stands ten feet tall, and has a heart the size of a man's head. Even the great clawed and fanged predators of the north step aside to let the moose pass.

Moose use waterways as travel routes and road maps, but basically go where they want. They pass through thick undergrowth as easily as a man's hand goes through the web of a spider.

The first Saturday in October is opening day of moose hunting in Ontario, but the exodus begins days earlier. Well before first light, caravans of pickup trucks hauling trailers and campers packed down with food, gear, and boats begin the long trek northward, in quest of the moose. Spirits are high in anticipation of what lies ahead.

The hunt for moose is more pilgrimage than vacation. You get recharged by the haunting power and spirit of the great boreal forests. The hunting grounds of northern Ontario lift your heart. But be prepared. They also take advantage of those who enter and relax their vigilance, even for an instant. It is a true wilderness.

The drive north from Kingston to our bush camp took about ten hours. We stopped once, for breakfast. During that stop, everyone talked about the dead Holstein cow we passed lying beside the highway. Everyone saw it except me.

"Anyone see the fox?" I asked. "It was running just off the road to the left about ten miles back near the construction site." This time, no one saw it except me. Someone asked if I knew what it meant to see a fox.

"Yes," I replied. "It means good luck hunting."

Hunting for moose is unlike hunting for other animals. A moose can't be pushed or driven through the woods to waiting hunters, nor is it baited. The early October northern woods are virtually impenetrable by man.

You can't go in, so you must get a moose to come out. You call it out, hoping that you see it before it sees you.

Imitating animal sounds and behaviour is a hunting technique developed ages ago. To call a moose, both hands are cupped over the nose and mouth; a deep breath is taken from as far down as you can reach. A mournful groan with a whine at its centre is released on the wind. Short calls and long calls are mixed in various sequences, each having a different meaning. To a nearby moose, it may sound like the pining of a lonely cow or the challenge of a rutting bull. It's frightening to hear one return the call. Their sound, like their bodies, is huge and primal. It's as if the ancient spirit of the northern forest has answered back.

You may need to do some additional coaxing to bring one out. Branches piled in advance are snapped by the hunter's foot to imitate the sound of an unseen moose thrashing and moving about. Water from a plastic bottle is poured slowly into a swamp to imitate a moose urinating while standing over open water.

When Francis calls, he imitates the sound of a female moose longing for attention. When the big bull heard the call that morning, he was somewhere across the swamp beyond the wooded shoreline far from view. He approached the call with caution. He wanted to see or smell the animal making that sound. He knew that to see it, he would have to walk into the open, and that meant possible danger. So he decided to get wind of it. That meant he would stay concealed and walk down his side of the swamp a safe distance away from the call. He wanted to approach the call from downwind, even if it meant walking all the way around the perimeter of the swamp. But as he walked along his side of the swamp, he began to think about something else.

The big bull made his fatal decision to take a shortcut across the swamp because something else besides losing his life began to worry him. He started to think the female moose he thought he had heard might be gone by the time he walked all the way around the swamp to get to her. When he stepped out from the safety of the woods and began crossing the swamp where it narrowed to 200 yards, he knew his life was at stake. By then his urge to mate had overcome his instinct to survive.

I watched him crossing. He hurried as he came. He knew he would only be in the open for a matter of seconds. He was two-thirds of the way across when I fired the first shot. I could tell that he knew he had made a terrible mistake. He stopped immediately. Then he started back. Then he stopped again after only a few steps. He knew the woods were too far away. He knew it was too late to turn back. He knew he had nowhere to go. The open space out in the swamp seemed to entangle him like a net.

While this was happening, I kept pounding him. I think my second shot broke his right front leg, which meant he couldn't lift his left front leg off the ground, which meant he couldn't move without falling down. He had to stand still. I fired six times.

Every good hunter has a conscience when it comes to killing. But if given the chance, he must try to give death the same way he would want to receive it: quickly and cleanly.

As I was killing him, I began to feel sorry for him. As I fired I knew he could not understand or even see what was killing him. As his great strength drained away into the swamp, he lowered his massive head and antlers. Then he fell. But he kept fighting until the end. It seemed the closer he came to death, the harder he struggled to escape it.

Down and free of the tremendous weight that had anchored him to the ground while he stood in the swamp, his four legs rose up in the air above the marsh hay and thrashed wildly all at once. He was still trying to get away. A few seconds later his legs sank from sight as he rolled from his back to his side. Finally his body came to rest, and I could no longer see him lying out there in the swamp. But then something else appeared above the marsh hay. It, too, was large and stationary and still. And when it glistened in the sunlight, it reminded me of a grave marker. It was his right antler.

The author and his big bull lying in the marsh hay after trying to take a shortcut across the swamp.

Eleven hours later, we got him back to the tent in two big pieces. It was eight-thirty at night. His head, his guts, and his legs from the knees down were left behind in the swamp where I had killed him.

The antlers of the big bull being raised in front of the army tent; author is second from right.

Two days later, we brought him to Kingston. When I arrived home late that night, I sat alone in my bathtub thinking about what had happened in that swamp. As I lowered my head beneath the water, I could see him again and smell him there with me.

His blood that had soaked into my hair now stained my bath water.

I remembered how I had felt sorry for him. Then I thought about what I had told everyone in the tent that night when we finally got back with the moose. I said, "We will all take a turn in the swamp."

A day will come when something will kill each of us. It may be something unexpected and unseen. It may even be something our big brains don't understand. We all won't grow old or get sick or become feeble. Some of us will die in our prime. Like that big bull.

When it happens, if we're lucky, something sudden will kill us. If we're not, it will take time. We won't go down and die crossing the swamp. We'll make it to the other side only to wish we hadn't.

CHAPTER 6

One of the best dogs that I ever hunted with was a beagle named Suzy. She was raised with a rabbit, and that's what made her such a good deer dog.

Hunting dogs by definition are hunters. They will at times hunt anything, including rabbits, which leave a scent trail and run fast and in circles when being pursued.

When a pack of hounds starts running a rabbit, the deer just slip away. But Suzy never ran rabbits. That's because she had bad memories of a rabbit and those memories stayed with Suzy all her life.

When she was born, a full-grown rabbit was put in Suzy's pen. Suzy tried to cuddle up to the rabbit for comfort and affection like any baby. But the rabbit, which was full-grown, wanted no part of her. Whenever Suzy came near, the rabbit kicked and pummeled her with its strong hind legs. Eventually, Suzy learned to leave the rabbit alone.

When Suzy got bigger, she was able to fight back, so the rabbit was taken away, but not entirely. The rabbit was put in a wire cage that sat on the mesh over Suzy's pen directly above the entrance to her doghouse. All day long, the rabbit shit and pissed on the entrance to Suzy's home.

When Suzy was old enough to go in the woods and hunt with the other dogs, she left the rabbits alone.

I entered the woods as I always have, the only way you can—disappearing into them the way a fish disappears, fading slowly from the surface into the deep. I was there this time not to hunt but to visit and say goodbye to an old friend.

As I walked among the trees, I remembered getting lost there once and doing what the experts tell you not to do. I panicked. Even worse, I didn't realize it. While I was panicking, I was spotted by someone watching from a distant ridge. But he didn't call out to me. He felt I had an important lesson to learn, one of many that the woods, the animals who live there, and the men and dogs who enter them each November would teach me.

I was lost for a long time that day before I saw with relief one of our hunting dogs, waving his crooked tail. It was Thunder. When I reversed my direction and followed him, he took me out of the woods and back to camp.

It was almost dark when Thunder and I arrived. The man who had watched me from the ridge was waiting. "One look and I knew you were lost," he said. Then came the lesson: "You shouldn't run through the woods. You might fall and hurt yourself, especially with a loaded gun. Besides, there's nothing in the woods to be afraid of."

I recalled his words as I approached my old friend. I knew he was just ahead, past the clover field, in the clearing behind the old camp, a log farmhouse hacked from the wilderness with bare hands and axes.

Then I saw him. His remains were scattered on the ground, the remains of the powerful hunting dog with that powerful name, Thunder. There was the empty skull that once held the yellow eyes, the moist nose and the enormous ears, that did the looking and found the scent and heard the deer. There were scattered bones from legs and paws that once hurt and bled but never quit when he ran deer. They knew him, as we did, by his howl.

He had run our deer through the cold dawns of eleven consecutive Novembers—twenty-two weeks in all. They were his deer, too, on our land, in his woods. He marked the chase by crying out, so we could see it in our listening and our memories, until we too become memories.

Thunder had been buried at the edge of the wilderness, maybe so he could always see it, near the site of the old camp, so he could see it, too, without a marker on his grave. I asked why, and Winnie told me: "I know where I buried him; that's what matters." But he had not been buried deep enough. The turkey vultures had found him, from high above at first, as they always do, by smell, marking his grave the way old Thunder found and marked deer.

The big birds had scratched at the earth and dug him up, using their claws and beaks like picks and shovels, then as knives and forks, to rip and tear Thunder's corpse to pieces. They watched over their shoulders the whole time for something watching them from inside the woods. And his blood became their blood and his flesh theirs. They flew away carrying some part of him to heights only a turkey vulture can soar to, heights old Thunder never dreamed of, if he dreamed of anything other than deer; if he even dreamed at all.

The highest tribute I can pay to Thunder, or any dog that ever growled, is that "He sired a better son." That son's name is Garth, and he hunted each November in the same big woods that he learned alongside Thunder, woods that Thunder had learned from his father, Blue, a purebred Bluetick hound. And so on, right back to the first hunting dog, a wolf, the first wolf that lay down in the warmth of a man's fire and was allowed to stay when it crept out of the cold, dark woods.

CHAPTER 7

Deer know dogs follow them by scent, just as deer detect and follow other animals, including man, by their scent.

A good dog will push the deer, not too fast and not too slow.

A big, strong, powerful dog turns the pursuit into a race. The deer and dog tear through the bush like two horses racing down a track. Deer win these races and exit your bush in a beeline; they may be miles and hours away before the dog loses them.

A slow dog unknowingly allows the deer to circle around behind it. The deer maintains a safe distance, and now it follows the dog. A good dog will "keep up the scare," crying out, telling the hunter the position and direction of the deer.

Smart deer get off their own scent trail. They take to water or double back and "jump off" the trail as a means of escape. Once, while standing on a ridge at the corner of a huge swamp, the dogs pushed a fox out past me. It darted across the shallow corner of the swamp, as did the dogs a few minutes later. The dogs called out all the while as the fox took them around the swamp again and passed me a second time. In fact, the dogs circled and crossed in front of me a third time but their prey was not ahead of them when they did.

The dogs had been outfoxed.

Dogs were the first domestic animals. Over the ages they have been changed to satisfy human needs. We have trained, bred, and refined them. We have given them names like people. Dogs are big business. Some have papers. We keep them as pets and have them as companions. Some wear knitted coats in the cold. Others play with little rubber toys and receive presents at Christmas.

But some dogs are different. We call them dogs but they aren't really dogs at all. I knew such an animal. He didn't bark. He howled. There was still a wolf inside him.

Turkey vultures dug up his father and tore his corpse to pieces. But when they carried him away, a part of his flesh and blood remained behind. Now his son Garth is dead, too.

I hunted with Garth for ten years. To the hunters of Verona and men from hunting camps in the surrounding area, Garth was a living legend comparable in size and strength to another fearless hunting dog named Lion, who emerged from the imagination of the famous American writer William Faulkner.

But Garth was a real hunting dog, as real as the game he ran and the vanishing woods he ran that game through; as real as the astonished men—including his owner, Gary Knox—who knew and talked of him, and the privileged ones who killed deer in front of him.

Garth could retrieve ducks and run bear and wolves, but it was his prowess as a deer hunter that earned him the title of "the wonder dog." When Gary arrived to hunt, Garth rode with him not as a dog rides, in a kennel in the box at the back of the truck, but as a friend does, up front in the seat beside Gary. During deer hunting season, visitors at The Terrible Ten camp would ask, as hunters always do, "How many you got hangin'?" meaning the deer carcasses on the meat pole. Eventually someone would turn to Gary and say, "How's the wonder dog doin'?"

That was his cue. From his chair at the head of the table, the one with his name scratched on the back, Gary would tell of Garth's role in each kill, and everyone would listen. He would tell where Garth had lifted deer, how far and how long he had run them, where he had brought them out, and to which hunters.

Garth standing over a small buck that he ran through the woods one morning. The deer was killed by the author.

But there were many nights when Gary wasn't there telling stories from his chair. Instead he was driving the back roads in the dark, visiting other camps, looking for Garth, who, most times, was still in the woods chasing deer. Gary often returned alone with the silent worried look of a parent missing a child. But sometimes he came back with another story to tell about how a camp miles away had kept and fed Garth after shooting a big buck in front of him. That's how the legend spread. Other camps shot deer in front of our dog.

Garth protected his territory at home in the small town of Verona. He once killed seven raccoons there at one time.

Raccoons are wild animals with big teeth and sharp claws. They can fight fiercely when they have to. Gary heard Garth fighting the raccoons, but by the time he got there they were all dead under a tree. Gary buried them nearby. The next day, Garth dug them up again.

Then there was Gary's new neighbour from the city and his pet Rottweiler that used to wander into Garth's backyard. The neighbour warned Gary that the Rottweiler was an attack dog. But attack dogs are from the city. The Rottweiler didn't know that Garth had never been to a city. It didn't realize that the wolf that had been bred and tamed out of its blood in the city was still inside Garth. It didn't know wolves even existed until the day it provoked Garth. Or maybe it just got too close that day.

Garth ripped half its face away so that it hung from the jawbone. Garth was tearing the attack dog from the city to pieces when Gary finally pulled him off.

Above all, Garth was a hunter, possessed by the will and ability to endure physical exhaustion and pain to pursue and catch and kill prey. When a deer crossed the old railway bed behind his doghouse, which was spiked to the ground, Garth dragged the doghouse into the woods with his chain and collar. Gary finally found him later all tangled up in the brush beside the tracks.

Garth's chest was as big as a man's. It held two huge lungs and the enormous heart that drove him. Running is what he did best—running through the woods with his nose low to the ground or high in the wind. He had a massive head, too. A blown-up photo of his head and face is still on the door to Gary's bedroom at the camp, where they often slept together like Lion and Boon Hogganbeck in Faulkner's story *The Bear*.

Garth lying in Gary's bunk as Gary looks on.

Inside The WILD

Now Gary keeps his ashes in a jar.

Before Garth's time, The Terrible Ten lost many deer that escaped from the chase by taking to water. They swam across Third Lake to a series of islands where they sat out the remainder of the hunting season. But unlike other dogs, Garth swam after them. He crossed Third Lake and forced the deer to swim back, where he resumed the chase, with a howl, on dry land where we waited with our guns.

In camp, Garth seemed like any other pet dog around home, snoozing by the fire or sitting blissfully while being patted and scratched. But he was different in the woods. I've seen what he did to deer that he caught even after they were dead. He was like a shark, then. His upper lip curled back, his long face wrinkled and his white teeth showed while he shook and tore and lifted a lifeless body twice the size of his own. When he got like that you just stood back and watched. I remember saying: "I wouldn't want that dog chasing or catching me even if I was dead."

I had reservations about writing Garth's story, even though I was a member of The Terrible Ten camp for fourteen good years. I hesitated because I left the camp when all but one member felt threatened by the truth about the blood and killing in my hunting stories. Gary Knox was not that one member who took my side.

But I know telling Garth's story is the right thing to do. I owe it to the dog and to the wolf that was inside him.

CHAPTER 8

On the last day of the moose hunt, two men were road hunting early in the morning. They were driving down a logging road to a turnaround area where a number of old skidder trails began. As they drove around a bend, they spotted a cow and calf standing just off the road about fifty yards away. The moose were looking right at the truck when it stopped.

Jimmy did most of the talking.

"Leave the headlights on and don't turn off the engine," he said, trying to be calm.

"Load your gun and put one in the chamber. But don't get out until we're both ready," he told the other man while snapping a full clip into his rifle.

"You take the one on the left and I'll take the one on the right," he added, never taking his eyes off the moose.

Then Jimmy turned and looked Dale in the face. "Are you ready?" he asked.

"I'm ready," Dale replied.

"Okay," Jimmy said, "get out and start shooting."

Seven seconds later, they were both dead.

To be successful at killing

When the dogger casts—or releases—the hounds from their leads, he follows behind as they disappear into the wind, which is the direction deer usually run when pushed by dogs. Ahead, hunters wait on watches forming the shape of a large pocket stretching across ridges, guts, and beaver dams. As the hounds push the deer toward the open spaces in front of the watches, the dogger tries to cut off the retreat by closing the pocket from behind.

When striking a scent trail, a dog doesn't bark. When the hair on the back of its neck rises and its voice cries out, it makes one of the few sounds loud enough to fill the November woods. It howls.

Howling is instinctive. It's been passed through the blood of generations of hunting dogs from the first dog. The moment a dog makes that sound—hunters call it "hound music"—it becomes wild again, like its great ancestor, the wolf, and the deer it is about to pursue.

The next move belongs to the deer. But first the deer must instinctively ask itself, "Was that howl for me?" If the answer is yes, the deer has only seconds to decide what to do. Hearing that sound, the deer pinpoints the location of the dogs. If the deer was moving or feeding, it stops. If it was lying down or resting, it stands.

The deer turns to face the sound of the dogs. The head tilts and the ears cock to get their direction, trying to determine if they are on its trail. The deer sniffs the wind with its head held high and slowly turning, from shoulder to shoulder. Finally, the deer starts to run, the white flag of its tail waving as it goes.

Instinct alone will guide it. Hiding or avoiding detection is what a deer does best, especially when being pursued.

To avoid detection, a deer does one of two things: it tries to outrun the dogs in a straight line, which often brings it past a hunter waiting to shoot it. Or the deer runs in circles trying to confuse its scent trail. Older, wiser deer, and bucks in particular, prefer circling and backtracking.

While dogging, I once watched a deer stop before jumping to the right, fifteen feet through the air across a stream. When the first hound arrived at the stream, it stopped and ran back along the scent trail, its nose to the ground. Then it made a series of circles while ranging out until it found the scent at the spot where the deer landed. The dog crossed the stream three times as it searched.

Why didn't I shoot? Hunters don't shoot at every deer they see. There is no sight more beautiful, graceful, and powerful in all of nature than a white-tailed buck stretched out in full flight using its feet as wings while weaving its way swiftly through the tangle of the autumn woods. If you have seen a deer this way, you will remember how, as

A deer "flying" through the woods.

suddenly as it appeared, with a flip of its tail, it was gone. I can't remember the number of times I have heard a hunter say, "That deer was flying through the woods."

The howl of a hound electrifies the woods. Everywhere there is a stirring of feet and a fluttering of wings as everything capable of moving tries to get out of the way of the chase.

A man possessed by fear often makes mistakes because he can't think clearly. But a wild animal that lives life as prey depends on fear. It's always afraid, even when there is no danger. And that means it's never afraid, not the way a man would be when the danger is real. Fear makes an animal alert and fast, and fleet and strong, because it uses fear to find a solution to the problem of staying alive.

The hunt is a contest where losing means loss of life and winning means bearing the burden of taking it. That means that hunting is neither a game, nor is it a sport. Hunting has become a recreation of a way of life once lived by our ancestors, but only those who were successful—those who failed, perished.

What determines the outcome of a hunt? Is it fate? Luck? The hounds? Or intelligence?

I believe instinct determines the outcome—the combined instincts of the deer, the dogs, and the hunter.

The hunter must awaken the instinct he once possessed and used but lost through reasoning instead of doing. A hunter achieves success not by raising himself above his prey but by lowering himself to its level.

A hunter will be successful only if he can do better what a deer does best. And he does it not just by imitating the animal he is trying to kill but by becoming an animal himself.

It happens the moment he sees the deer that he has followed in the voice of the hounds. It happens because the deer does not see him. It happens if the hunter avoids detection. It happens while he is standing still, and waiting, even hiding, letting the deer approach a hidden danger it knows is there.

A hunter becomes like an animal when he stops thinking and no longer tries to reason to find a rational solution, because he must stop thinking to raise his gun. He must not be afraid to kill, or waver when the time comes to pull that trigger, even though his thoughts have been racing around inside him with anticipation as the chase moves unseen but not unheard inside the woods energized by its sound.

If the hunter is successful, he won't hear the gun fire, or see its flash, or feel its jolt against his shoulder.

When the hunt ends and he is successful, he may realize he was never interested in killing, but only in doing the things he had to do to prepare himself to kill. This means becoming an animal again, which is what he always has been but never knew until the moment came when he must deliver death.

CHAPTER 9

Deer don't die pretty. Death is always ugly in the November woods.

One morning I shot a six-point buck trying to cross a beaver dam. I could hear the sound of snapping branches and pounding hooves before he broke out of the woods into the opening near the dam. I could hear him panting and see his breath as he was crossing the dam.

He didn't see me until the moment I started pulling the trigger. I was ten feet away and could see his eyes bulge just before I shot him.

He jumped sideways when the first bullet hit him and tore a big hole behind his front shoulder. He stumbled but kept running. I could see he was not moving right and was hit bad. About fifty feet away, he crouched on the ground behind a juniper bush.

Just before I fired again, he looked around the bush at me, and I thought how he looked like a big dog. I hit him again with the second shot but he managed to get up and go another fifty feet. He was dead when I walked up to him. From the size of the hole in his side I knew I had hit him in the same spot both times.

I followed his blood trail back to the juniper bush where he had been hiding. Both his kidneys were there on the ground. He ran that last fifty feet without them.

"DADDY, HOW CAN YOU KILL BAMBI?"

Over time, hunters learned to speak the language of animals. They discovered that certain sounds or calls possessed the power to charm wild animals. The skill was passed on by word of mouth.

Today, imitating animal sounds to deceive and kill remains hunting's dark art. Many animals die because they were talked into it.

Years ago, the art of calling was revealed to me on the eve of opening day of moose hunting. We were huddled at our fire eating stew on a cold, black October night, as other campfires burned in the Northern Ontario wilderness like distant stars scattered across its vast, extravagant sky.

I learned how to lure a cow moose and her calf from hiding by making a series of loud groans and soft grunts while cupping my hands over my mouth and nose. I learned how to imitate the distress call of a confused calf crying, "Where are you? I'm frightened," and the reassuring sound of a cow answering, "Everything is all right, you can come out now."

Cows and calves travel in pairs. From the time the calf is born in some secluded hideaway, they are inseparable. Their bond is formed with affection and nurtured by trust and dependence. If one is shot and the other is not, a hunter waiting in the shadows near the dead body will call out, manipulating the fear of a worried cow or frightened calf, luring the animal back into the open by making it think its child or mother is still alive.

I heard a story about a mother moose whose calf had been shot dead. Torn between instincts of self-preservation and motherhood, she returned to the kill site on her own, without being called, refusing to abandon her dead calf. The hunters didn't have a cow tag licence, so she was scared off repeatedly with warning shots as her calf was quickly gutted. Later, she jumped in the water and swam after the boat as it hauled her calf down the river.

A bull moose is deceived with a different sound, one irresistible to those possessed by the devil of hot desire. This happened to a bull moose somewhere up the Spanish River, beyond the northern end of Lake Huron. It was at a beaver pond surrounded by green pine trees.

The bull was coaxed down a forested slope into the open by a hunter imitating the bellowing of a lonely cow. The first hurried shots missed and he retreated in fear to the safety of the forest. But his blood was up. A series of short, croaking grunts got his attention, making him think another bull had suddenly appeared. Minutes later, the same high, wide-swaying rack of antlers reappeared in the undergrowth as he crashed through to the edge of the pond, ready for battle.

Betrayed by his own instinct, the forest seemed to give him up. He stopped, it seemed, for a last, deliberate, backward glance as a gun was raised from across the pond. When he turned again to face the other side, lightning flashed and thunder crashed. He managed a half step to the left before wavering. He fell not as you would expect—sideways with a loud crash and a big bounce like a tree. Instead, his legs buckled and he collapsed quietly, as if some powerful unseen hand had reached up and pulled him down.

For some, hunting has become too easy, too predictable, or too ugly, darkened by images of a concerned mother and a helpless child called out of hiding. There was a time when hunting required no explanation. Then attitudes began to change when the myth of the bloodthirsty hunter was born. The year was 1942. It happened in a make-believe place called "the wonderful world of Disney."

A single image was the catalyst. It was a motherless child. More than a half-century later, the most common question still asked of hunters is: "How can you kill Bambi?" My daughter asked me that question when she was five years old. I am compelled to answer.

Why do men hunt? Do they enjoy killing animals? Surely, it would be easier to buy an axe and raise chickens. Maybe that's something we should all do at least once so we think about the meat we eat and where it comes from. No, I don't believe we hunt to kill.

So do we hunt for sport? Hunters know that guns are no match against the eyes, ears, noses, and legs of wild animals. I could argue that through the technology of the gun we have not taken advantage but given it away, because we rely too much on guns and not on our senses.

Perhaps we hunt for camaraderie and friendship. It's true that the companionship and rituals of hunting are as important as the hunt itself. After we clean up and shut down our hunting camp each season, we always end our time together with handshakes and even a few hugs before heading out. But these things also can be found at a hockey rink or in the locker room.

The author holding his young daughter, Abbey;
a deer hangs from a tree beside them.

Do we hunt because we love nature? Nature can be enjoyed without carrying a gun. But hunters don't want to just look at nature. We want to become part of it. For two short weeks, we want to become like the ancient people who first called the animals, because some small portion of that wildness is still in our blood.

Hunters love nature and the animals whose blood they spill, as I love my only child and daughter, whose blood is my own.

Hunting is something I cherish and want to protect. It is part of my emotion, intellect, and reason for living. It gives me a soul and a spiritual being. It is a reminder of who I am and where I came from. Hunting is perfectly natural. It needs no defence.

Those who oppose hunting deny their own humanity. Our human character was formed in the hunting and gathering stage of evolution. Hunting is the foundation of humankind. We are all the descendants of successful hunter-gatherers.

All men still hunt something. Some hunt wild animals and others hunt for cars, or clothes, or just to collect things.

There are men who even hunt in their homes, from their couches. Sometimes a woman sits nearby watching. They raise their arms and point their weapons at a television set. It's an obsession. They don't pull a trigger; they press a button. They sit searching frantically with their eyes, firing at everything they see—click, click, click, goes the channel-changer.

And what is it they hunt? Mostly naked women and acts of violence.

On that same moose-hunting trip in Northern Ontario, seven of us hunted out of a tent for a week. We shared a single tag for one bull moose. We saw four cows up close that week and didn't fire a single shot.

We weren't there to kill. That's why it's called hunting.

CHAPTER 10

My moose-hunting partner shot a big bull. It was a crisp morning and we were walking to our watches when he spotted the bull. He shot it while I stood there beside him.

We were hunting deep inside a primordial forest of the Canadian Shield in northern Ontario, a place you can't get to in a truck, boat, or even a four-wheeler.

When the bull went down, we walked over to look at it. When I got up close I blurted out, "Look at the size of it!" There was no response. I turned and saw him standing about twenty feet behind me, punching a series of numbers into a cell phone, which I didn't know he had.

"What are you doing?" I asked in disbelief.

He said, "I'm phoning my wife back home in Kingston to tell her that I just shot a moose."

I was so angry inside that I felt like shooting him. But the phone didn't work and I didn't say a word.

SPARING LIFE

When compassion stalks the hunter, he gives an animal its life by choosing not to kill when he can.

A true act of compassion is spontaneous. It is not a calculated reason for holding back, such as not having a game tag or not having a clean shot. Sometimes a hunter gets "buck fever." He is so overcome by excitement at the sight of a deer, he forgets himself and does not shoot. While deer hunting one fall, I chose to give life.

Most hunters can tell you every minute detail about every big game animal they have ever killed. They remember the time, place, weather, number of shots, distance, and how fast and far the animal ran before it collapsed and died. In twenty years of hunting, I have killed ten deer and three moose.

I killed my first deer on my first day of hunting. It happened near the railway tracks that ran through the middle of the woods where we hunted. A lot of deer and dogs lost their lives on those tracks after being hit by trains.

But not this deer. Pursued by hounds and panic, he crossed a railway line and bounded up a small knoll where I stood pointing a loaded shotgun at his head.

Though he came within nine footsteps—I paced them off later—he never saw me waiting. He was not surprised by my presence or the boom of the gun, but rather to find death suddenly inside him, as he flipped backwards and tumbled down the hill into the ditch beside the tracks. He barely lifted his head and looked back across his shoulder at me, before releasing one long last sigh. Then his tongue relaxed and hung limply from the side of his mouth. He did not feel the teeth of the hounds that tore into him.

His head still hangs mounted on my office wall at home, looking over and past my right shoulder when I sit and write. His keen senses, which had always kept him safe from danger, failed him when he needed them most. In death, he appears poised and attentive, but his big eyes stare at nothing, his flaring nostrils receive no messages and his erect ears are filled with emptiness.

I've never heard a hunter admit to sparing an animal out of compassion, maybe because it's not manly. But if I have done it, then others have, too.

The morning it happened, I sat on my watch filled with sorrow caused by recent events in my life. It left me feeling limp, like that deer by the tracks, and hollow inside, like his head on my wall. Unlike the deer, sorrow made me feel the teeth of the hounds.

Just after dawn, a doe and fawn stepped out of cover about a hundred yards away and walked slowly along a creek bed about twenty yards to my right. When the doe stopped to look back at her fawn, which was feeding with its head down, I lifted my rifle, fixing the crosshairs inches behind her shoulder. I followed her through the scope

Two beagle brothers and a buck run over by separate trains during hunting season. The beagles each had an ear tattooed when their owner insured them. To make the insurance claim, he cut those ears off with a knife when they died on the tracks. Coyotes got to the buck; we found him partly eaten.

until she stopped, within thirty yards of me. She was still unaware that death was near.

But I did not fire. I lowered the gun. Both deer froze at my sudden movement. Their eyes bulged and ears cocked in my direction, as their noses found me.

They seemed to sense no danger, perhaps realizing it had already passed. Quietly, they turned away, without looking back, and disappeared into the safety of the November woods. Sparing the doe, a protector and teacher, meant sparing her fawn, who would surely die later, alone, as winter descended and food became scarce and hard to find. Only wolves or coyotes, who know much about hunger and nothing of mercy, could provide a more merciful end.

Why didn't I shoot? Because this time I didn't see two wild animals—a doe and fawn; I saw a mother and child, needing each other. I didn't shoot because I didn't want either of them to feel the pain I was feeling.

I often think back to that moment and time, then forward, to the lives of the two deer. I didn't kill them that day because of the compassion I felt.

Perhaps one day I will see them again.

CHAPTER 11

The way to hunt is for as long as you live against as long as there is such and such an animal.

Ernest Hemingway, Green Hills of Africa

IT HAPPENED BECAUSE HE WANTED TO HUNT

If it had been a moose and dead, we would have gutted and dragged it from the woods. But it was a man and he was alive, so we covered and carried him.

It took six of us to get him out of the woods and back to the logging road. There had been an accident. We thought he was dying. He had shouted, "Let me die, let me die!" A rescue helicopter came and hovered over us as we stood around him where he had fallen. But there was no place safe to land. So we carried him on a stretcher almost a mile through the bush to the logging road where an ambulance waited to take him to the hospital in Espanola.

It happened on the morning of opening day of moose hunting. When the ambulance drove away, half the day was gone and we hadn't even started hunting.

On the night before, a hunter from another camp had visited our tent and told us that he had seen in the headlights of his truck a big bull crossing the logging road near a hydro line.

"I know where that moose will be in the morning," I said. "There's a big open meadow with a creek running through it that's not far from the road and the hydro line. I've hunted there before. I know how to find the meadow."

"Why don't you and I go there tomorrow?" asked the Frenchman, who was a recent addition to our camp.

"Okay," I replied.

But when tomorrow arrived, our hunt was delayed because of the accident, and now I was in a hurry to get going. It was almost noon when we all returned to our camp.

"I'll be ready to leave the tent in ten minutes," I said, looking directly at the Frenchman. "We've already lost a half day because of the accident."

"Don't I have time to relax and have a cup of coffee and eat a sandwich first?" he asked.

"No. It's time to hunt."

"But this is a vacation for me. I'm tired, too. What's the big rush?" he asked.

"We're here to hunt. Besides, you will never have a better chance to kill a moose than you will today," I told him.

The Frenchman and I left ten minutes later.

We stopped on the way only to erase the tracks where the big bull had crossed the road the night before. We didn't want road hunters to see them, because they are not hunters at all.

They hunt from trucks while driving the back roads. Road hunters rank even below those who pay to kill on game farms, where hunting is more like playing a video game with real guns and live animals. Real hunting happens inside the wilderness. Game farms are surrounded by fences. The animals can't escape. The owner/operators of game reserves guarantee success—the only way you can—for a price. Real hunting requires uncertainty.

When the Frenchman and I found the open meadow, I put him on a watch where the treeline met the meadow. He could stand in the shadows of the pine trees behind him and see the sunlit open space surrounding the creek in front. I would have stayed there if I had been alone, because I knew it was the best spot to kill a moose.

I left him there partly because I knew he had never been in that part of the woods before, partly because he had never killed a moose by himself, and partly because I am not a killer—a hunter who considers his hunting trip a success only if he kills.

But the main reason I left him there was because, unlike the others who stayed in the tent drinking, the Frenchman wanted to hunt. As I sat at my watch that afternoon, I realized that's all I have ever wanted to do. And I remembered a time when I was the one who didn't know the woods. I was the one who had never killed a wild animal. So I had to wait for others to show me the way because, as every good hunter will tell you, the secret to success as a hunter is knowing the woods. With time and careful study you learn to read the wilderness and where it opens like at that meadow, and where it closes and becomes overgrown and impassable, and where it gets steep and becomes shallow, and where it disappears into dark holes and beneath swamps, and where it narrows at beaver dams and on game trails, and most importantly, where it all comes together and begins to finally make sense at a place located somewhere deep inside your mind.

But there were many times that I waited in vain to go out and hunt. That's because I hunted with men who had stopped being hunters. They preferred to sit inside and drink together. They made excuses not to hunt. It was either too early or too late. Or it was too hot or too cold. And sometimes it was too windy or too wet. The truth is that they were too drunk and too lazy.

The Frenchman and his record moose lying in the meadow where he shot it.

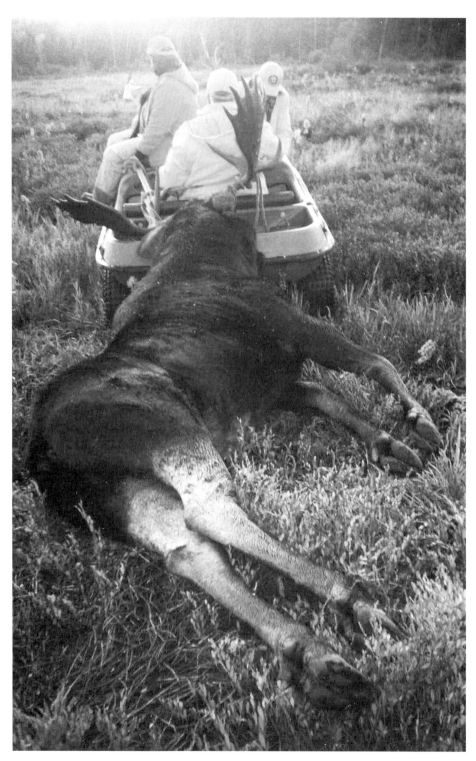

The Frenchman's moose being dragged from the woods.

Inside The WILD

Suddenly my thoughts were interrupted. The unmistakable sound of a rifle being fired nearby made me stand up instantly. I pressed my forefinger gently against the safety just above the trigger guard on my rifle while my eyes and ears searched frantically for movement. The other rifle kept banging away. I counted the shots. There were nine. It was the Frenchman.

Unlike the man on the stretcher who was carried a mile through the woods that morning in an hour, it took hours to move the Frenchman's moose even a few hundred yards. That's because it was the biggest moose that any of us had ever seen. The big bull weighed 1,550 pounds and was entered in the Ontario Big Game Record Book because its rack scored 169 5/8 points.

An amphibious all-terrain, off-road vehicle called an Argo was winched to a pair of four-wheelers to drag the moose across the meadow, through the creek, and up a ridge.

An Indian from a nearby camp came to help get the moose back to our tent. It was already gutted when he arrived.

"Who did that?" he asked.

"I did," I said.

"Never seen a cut like that before. What are ya, some kinda doctor?" he asked.

He was referring to the large incision that left a long rectangular space where the bull's throat and windpipe once were. It is not an exaggeration to say a moose's windpipe is almost as big as a dryer hose. This one looked like that lying on the ground all bloodied and fully intact.

Most hunters tear out the windpipe to air out the animal. This is done by reaching with your hands up through the body cavity after the moose has been gutted. We had turned the moose over on its back to make it easier to gut. After the Frenchman opened it and started taking its insides out, I removed the windpipe by cutting the area beneath his chin down to his chest where I knew the windpipe would be.

I took the Indian's remark as a compliment because Indians are renowned hunters.

Later, while we dragged the moose from the meadow, he said, "If you ever get an Indian to tag your moose, don't just switch guns with him—make sure you trade cigarettes, too. If the game warden comes along, he may ask the Indian to show him the place the moose was shot from. The warden will check for empty shell cartridges and cigarette butts on the ground. If the Indian says he shot the moose instead of you, he better be carrying your gun and smoking your brand of cigarettes."

It was nine-thirty at night before we got the moose out to a truck on the same logging road where the ambulance had waited that morning. The Frenchman was a happy man that day. He was proud, too, because he had called the big bull out. He told us the story again and again. And we listened because he had earned our attention.

But that was only part of his reward. He will never forget that day. He will think of it often and smile whenever he does. He will tell that story as long as he hunts, probably as long as he lives. And he will know in his heart that it all happened because he wanted to hunt.

Knowing he knows will be my reward.

CHAPTER 12

Francis Pixley is the best hunter I have had the honour of hunting with. He taught me a lot about calling moose, reading their signs, and understanding how they behave.

I'll never forget one simple but extraordinary display of tracking by Francis. He was following fresh moose prints with well-defined sharp edges at the top and empty bottoms. As he walked quietly along, he noticed various places where the moose had nibbled on birch, poplar and maple, picking the branches clean of leaves and breaking stems and twigs so the severed and still-white ends showed.

Francis knew he was following a cow from the size and shape of the print. Francis was sure he would spot the cow because it was feeding and moving slowly.

Then he noticed a sign that told him the moose was only a matter of yards away. On a small maple where the moose had fed, all but one of the remaining leaves had frost on it. The frost had just been melted by the warm breath of the moose that had just been browsing.

Francis walked over the next small rise, and saw the moose standing broadside forty yards away.

Francis used to say, "Look at everything around you. Hunting is looking. Look and the woods will speak to you."

When I first began hunting it seemed that I usually spent a whole week in the bush from dawn to dusk waiting for a single chance that came and went in a matter of a few seconds. Whenever I saw a deer in the woods, it was already running away. The deer always managed to see me first.

That's because deer are preoccupied with looking. For them, danger and death are lurking everywhere. And deer don't just look with their eyes. They often find you with their noses and ears. When they find you this way, you never see them at all.

Deer are masterful lookers. A deer will stand perfectly still and watch you walk past sometimes within a few feet. It won't move until it thinks you've seen it. While it watches you, it looks at your eyes. But once you make eye contact or turn its way, a deer will raise its tail slowly before leaping away and crashing off into the woods.

I have learned to walk at times to within ten yards of a deer in the woods that was watching me. I approached it by not making eye contact or even looking its way while slowly veering towards but never directly at it. As long as the deer feels you haven't seen it and that you are going to walk past it, the deer will often stay still and let you pass.

To find deer you must learn to out-look them. It's difficult to out-look a deer in the woods. You must look for small details like the still-white end of a broken twig, and at the big picture, like the lay of the land. You must learn to look as far as the eye can see and be able to focus on some small, still shape that appears at a distance to be part of the landscape. You must look while walking, standing, sitting, and climbing. Above all, you must discipline yourself to avoid not looking.

The art of looking is the essence of hunting. There can be no hunting without it. The woods are full of telltale signs that reveal much about habits of the animals that act upon them. Lodges and burrows and nests show where they live. Gnawed limbs and clipped leaves and stripped bark show what they eat. Tracks in dust and mud and snow show where they travel.

Looking at the woods has helped me understand the animals that spend their lives inside them. By looking closely, I have been gradually drawn into a world that is unseen and feared by most people. By looking carefully at the woods, I have been provided with a glimpse into the minds of the animals that depend upon them. Eventually I even began to think like a wild animal. And by doing that I discovered that I have wild animal spirit of my own.

You must feel at home in the woods to become good at looking for deer. You must learn where to look for game trails and deer beds. You must learn how to spot territorial markers like scrapes and rubs. You must learn how to read tracks and droppings so you will know when deer are around without seeing them. When you learn to find deer this way, you will eventually see one down the barrel of your gun before it sees you—if it ever sees you at all.

Wild animals are shy and quiet and secretive. Many are nocturnal, which means they become active during the night when they are more difficult to see. Animals recognize tracks left by other animals but they are so highly evolved that most detect and track each other by scent. If you have been fortunate enough to hunt alongside a beagle or hound you will often see one stick its nose deep into a set of tracks to identify not only what kind of animal it's following but how long ago that animal passed. If you spend time hiking or backpacking through the woods, stop and turn around and wait quietly. You may see a deer walking along behind you with its nose to the ground following your scent trail. I surprised a doe doing this one November morning.

In the wilderness, "looks" can kill. It's fitting that you raise a rifle to your eye for your last look at a deer before pulling the trigger. In that final moment, the gun becomes an extension of your eye. Often during that last and most important look of all, some hunters begin shaking and become too nervous to shoot. I believe it's because their conscience is telling them not to shoot. Killing animals is not for everyone. It's not something people do every day. Most people pay in the supermarket for the deaths of the animals they consume. They condone killing but prefer to look away.

To be a hunter, you must have a clear conscience about killing and possess the will to kill. Sometimes the will comes from necessity. But most hunters don't kill because they have to. They kill because it gives them some sort of pleasure. Otherwise they wouldn't do it.

That pleasure is the focus of the anti-hunter. They do not oppose killing. They oppose the pleasure it provides.

Some hunters get that pleasure from the glory they receive from their peers after they are successful at killing. Others enjoy feeling powerful because they have killed. Killing for glory and power may be questionable to some people. But these hunters kill what they eat, which means that when the time comes they don't look away.

There is one other group of hunters. They want to go beyond just looking at the wilderness and watching wild animals. They want to become part of that world and like those animals. That's what gives them pleasure. And for them, killing is as natural as being in the woods and looking for the wild game that they have come to pursue.

CHAPTER 13

"Give me some moose meat," my friend said. "I'm going to make you some vadas.*"*

"What's that?" I asked.

"Vadas is Hungarian for 'wild' and the name of my mother's recipe for cooking game. It has a delicious sauce and she made it to prepare all the animals my old man killed—deer, moose, prairie chicken, duck, rabbit, and, best of all, snow goose.

"Back in Hungary she used the same recipe to cook wild boar that the old man shot illegally with the gamekeeper on the nearby estate of the former Prince Esterhazy. That was during the darkest communist years of the early 1950s when it was a crime to own a gun and hunt.

"That's why the first thing he bought himself in Canada was a shotgun."

So I gave him a big chunk of prime moose meat we had just brought back from Northern Ontario. It hadn't even been frozen.

My friend spent an entire Saturday afternoon making the dish: cutting, slicing, spicing, and simmering the meat and sauce. When he invited me over to eat some, he apologized because he had only a little left. His wife and daughter had eaten most of it.

His twelve-year-old daughter is an animal lover, moved to tears by suffering animals and revolted by hunting. Yet she gorged herself on the moose and used thick slices of bread to wipe her plate clean.

The wind blew in our faces that morning and in our favour. As a result, we saw them seconds before they saw us. Two moose stood side by side, as we did, fifty yards away. We stared at each other through the bare branches of a bent birch tree growing out of a shallow ravine that ran between us.

The cow moved first, shifting her head slightly to the left for a better look, as if trying to confirm what she was seeing but not believing. Then her head swung slowly right towards the bull with a look that seemed to say, "Do you see them, too?"

All this looking took only a few seconds. When the cow's head turned back in our direction our guns were up. The banging began immediately. They were surprised again. This time by death. It was inside them.

The first raven appeared before the gutting was done. The cow was full of fresh droppings, and I squeezed them out through the intestines of her open body cavity into a pile on the soft grey moss that covered the ground between my knees.

Someone returned to the kill site the next day and saw that the two blood-soaked gut piles had disappeared. They were in the bellies of the timber wolves that had eaten them. Life in wild places depends on listening, and they knew where to look, not just from the sound of the guns but by the "KRRRAAaaah" of the ravens. All that remained were the droppings from the cow.

Hunting doesn't end when the prey is killed; hunting ends a short time later when a wild predator begins eating whatever it has brought down. But a human hunter does something very different. Alone with the animal he has killed from a distance, he performs a silent ritual to show he has conquered and taken possession of his prey. He kneels and touches it with his hands.

As he studies and admires his prey up close, he lifts and moves the head by the antlers to count the points, if it's a bull or buck. He will always search with his hands for the small, round, blood-stained hole where the bullet entered the animal and the large, ragged one where it left, because death in the wilderness always attracts a crowd, and the next hunter who arrives, and everyone after, will ask, "Where is it hit?"

I have examined dead animals this way with my hands and eyes. I am often surprised by little things I find, like the green stains on the hair between the hooves of a moose, or the small, white patch on the chest of the black bear, or the scent glands in the corners of the eyes of a white-tailed buck.

The laying on of hands symbolizes completion of a successful hunt because a man who becomes a hunter can never touch a wild animal while it lives. The moment he touches his prey, it is no longer prey, or even an animal. It's meat.

With that touch, he stops being a hunter, and by that I mean an animal, too, and a predator also, because that's what a hunter is. Instead he becomes a man again which, at its best, is many things, the worst of which is a consumer—that part of each of us that consumes and destroys the world we live in by poisoning its air, staining its water, and disfiguring its land.

Photo showing the moment a wild animal becomes meat.

There is honour in everything you do as a hunter, and must do after a kill as a man if you are successful as a hunter. Anyone who has hunted has heard it said many times: "Once the animal is down, the work begins." That work has a single goal: preserving and preparing meat for eating.

A dead moose comes out of the bush in one of two ways: quartered and carried piece by piece, or dragged whole behind a four-wheeler or boat.

Deer are handled differently. After a deer is gutted in the bush, two hunters drag it out. If it's a buck, the antlers are used as handles for dragging. If it's a doe, a stick about an inch thick and a foot long is used. First the membrane between the doe's nostrils and the tendons above its front hooves are slit open with a knife. Then one end of the stick is sharpened and forced through the slits. The stick is pushed through the tendon of one leg, then through the membrane at the tip of the nose before being jammed through the tendon of the other leg. Its hooves are forced down the length of the stick until they touch each side of its nose. The doe looks like it's praying as the hunters pull it through the woods after grabbing the ends of the stick. The heart and liver are put back in the body cavity before the drag-out.

At least one wolf that feasted on those gut piles that morning followed the blood trail and tufts of hair left behind the four-wheelers that dragged those moose to the canvas tent that was our camp. The wolf's howling woke us during the night.

The hide of a wild animal is removed by two or three men working together using short, sharp, skinning knives, which they often wear on their belts while hunting. A big game animal is hung head down and whole with ropes, pulleys, and hooks for up to two weeks from a tree branch, from a meat pole, or in a cooler, to stretch, tenderize, and drain the blood from its meat.

After it's quartered and beheaded with a meat saw or axe, its body is flushed clean with fresh water. Each quarter is covered in plastic before being transported home in a truck or trailer.

Some hunters butcher their own meat. Steaks, chops, roasts and stewing meat are cut, wrapped, taped, identified, dated, and distributed evenly to everyone in the hunting party. The division of meat is the final ritual of the hunt and normally occurs in front of everyone.

It's illegal to sell wild meat, so consumers can't buy it. Hunters call it "God's meat," not because He liked to eat it but because it has remained as wild and free and pure as the day He gave it breath and blood and bone.

The only way you can have a taste is to kill or receive it as a gift. Wild meat is often shared with friends, especially other hunters who were unsuccessful. Some people, and women in particular, who grew up on wild meat provided by their fathers, often ask hunters if they can spare a piece if there's any extra. They usually say, "I remember how good it tasted," or "I still have my mother's recipe."

Whenever our hunting gang kills a moose, I save a few packages in my freezer to make a moose stew for the first night of our next hunting trip. A year later, some part of that moose always makes the round trip back home and is returned to its birthplace in the northern Ontario wilderness, after passing through our bodies one last time.

When we eat the last of our wild meat in camp, the story of the cow and the bull, and the ravens and the wolves is retold. Our words recount not only how it was killed, and how it was gutted, dragged, hung, skinned, quartered, beheaded, butchered, wrapped, and cooked, but how it tasted, and that nothing was wasted, not even the pile of droppings that returned to the earth beneath the soft grey moss that still covers the ground somewhere inside the northern woods where two wild animals became meat.

A bull moose is being broken and processed into meat.
The photos illustrate the steps from the gutting of the moose to the making of some of it into sausage.

The big bull moose after being gutted.

The bull being dragged through the woods with a four-wheeler.
The chain saw is used to cut a trail.

A hunter shinnying up a tree to help get a rope over a high branch to
hang the moose, which is now in the back of the truck. Notice man
standing ready with rope.

The moose being hoisted into the tree.

The author removing tenderloins before hanging the moose in the tree.

The author posing with moose and rifle.

The moose after it is skinned.

One of our moose-hunting gang making moose sausage.

CHAPTER 14

*During the eighteenth century, the great composer
Wolfgang Amadeus Mozart wrote a letter to his father
describing a new composition. He said, "Here and there,
only the connoisseur can derive satisfaction, but in such
a way that the non-connoisseur will be pleased, without
knowing why."*

THE CAMP COOK AND THE GREAT COMPOSER

I was listening to music one night when my doorbell rang. It was a
surprise visit, but I knew who it was by the sound of the bell.

I know only one man who holds his finger on the button until you
answer. When I opened the door, he said, "Hey lad, how ya doin'?" It

Fred setting up his kitchen on one of our early moose-hunting trips.

was Fred, one of my hunting buddies from Verona, and his wife, Doris, who had driven them into town.

Fred is our cook at the hunting camp and a true Verona boy.

He owns a big pickup truck and wears an assortment of ball caps that change with the seasons. He usually has one with an image of a largemouth bass or white-tailed buck over the peak. He has his own way of talking, too. We drove together one time on a moose-hunting trip up around Espanola. We passed through Oshawa during rush hour. When he saw all the traffic he said, "There's a lot of drive on the road."

When he arrives for a visit, Fred often comes through the door with a small beer cooler in one hand and an open beer in the other. His blood, unlike the blood of most men, is not fully tamed. He is like a dog that is half-dog and half-wolf. The day after deer hunting ends, he starts thinking about next year.

As soon as he got inside my house he laughed and asked, "What the hell is that."

"Do you like it?" I asked in return.

"You're gettin' weird, son. Get some real music on. That's crap," he said.

"Weird is good," I answered.

"Did you hear what he said there, Doris? I told ya he's losin' it."

We all went into the kitchen to sit and talk. In the past, whenever Fred complained about my music, I'd usually put on some country and western or stuff from the 1950s, which I knew he liked. But this time I let my music play. It was an opera about a tale of mistaken identity, hatred and unfulfilled love, called *Il Trovatore*. It was composed in 1853 by the Italian master Giuseppe Verdi.

Fred is a hard worker. Like all hard workers, he never seems to stop, because he likes working. It's what people always say about him and something he will be remembered for. I have worked alongside Fred many times, for long hours, mostly as his go-boy while building our hunting camp or putting another extension on his garage. He'd hand me a hammer and a pouch full of nails and declare: "I'll make a carpenter out of you if it kills me." When I did something wrong, he would ask: "Don't you know anything?"

Fred seems happiest when he works. When he gets in a real groove while measuring boards, sawing lumber, and hammering nails, he starts to whistle. He doesn't actually whistle any kind of recognizable tune. He doesn't even seem to know he's whistling. He just whistles away as if in some trance-like state or private world.

"Are you enjoying your retirement?" I asked him.

"I'm busier now than I've ever been."

"Have you been back to the plant for a visit?"

"What fer?"

Fred sat with his back to the music as we talked. Then a chorus of male voices began to sing, "*All'opra! All'opra! Daglia martella!*" ("To work! To work! Hammer away!") The gypsies in the opera were awakening to a new day in their mountain encampment in Spain. The famous piece known as "the anvil chorus" began as they seized their hammers and set to work singing at the fire of their forges.

As their hammers continued to ring rhythmically on anvils, and the music and voices rose and fell in time with the blows, Fred's head made a slow quarter turn to the right, towards the music. But this was an opera and, like many operas, it was sung in Italian, and Fred didn't understand the words.

But no translation was necessary. He knew what those men were doing, and how they felt inside.

We continued talking as the voices sang and the music played and the hammers rang on the anvils. Then something happened that took me by surprise. Fred began to whistle.

It was that same tuneless whistle I had heard when we worked together. It came out of him as it had so often before, of its own volition, for its own pleasure. This time, it was the music of an Italian opera that had reached out and touched him, acting upon him, forcing him to respond and react to it.

When Fred goes home, he likes to leave an empty beer bottle on my front lawn or a beer cap in my driveway. It's his sign, a message that means we're friends. It's as if he's leaving a calling card or giving me a little gift.

But his present to me that night was hearing him whistle, just after his head made that slow quarter turn towards Verdi's music.

CHAPTER 15

Re: L.W. Oakley's column on taxidermy ("Wildlife transformed into art," April 20).

"I have news for Oakley: Hanging a dead animal's head on your wall isn't art. It's a statement that says, 'I need to kill something to feel important.' It announces to the world that with a mere movement of my trigger finger, I can make something significant happen—at a safe distance, of course.

"Perhaps it's a stretch to suggest that sticking a poor deer's head on your rec room wall is only a few notches above the medieval practice of impaling a petty thief's head on a pike at the city gates in order to send a message from those who get a buzz from being in power."

Published letter to the editor in The Kingston Whig-Standard *on April 28, 2005, from Fraser Petrick of Kingston, Ontario.*

Mount of two big bucks created by World Champion Taxidermist Len Murphy of Baltimore, Ontario. The piece is entitled "Living on the Edge." Both bucks were shot in 2003 during the same week by Jerry Moore, a member of our hunting camp. The nervous deer on the right has his ears pinned back and is ready to bolt.

Almost a year had passed since we first met last fall. I had thought of him often during that time. In an hour I would see him again and as I drove along the highway I wondered if he would look the same.

I didn't recognize him immediately. That surprised me, because he looked exactly the same as he did the first time I saw him.

When I arrived I parked and walked into the shop of professional taxidermist Bill Warren in Landsdowne, Ontario.

When I introduced myself, he asked me, "Do you know which one is yours?"

I took a few moments before answering because I was overwhelmed by what I saw: the antlers, heads, necks, chests, and shoulders of about thirty lifelike white-tailed bucks mounted on the walls.

Then I pointed and said, "That one."

He smiled. "No. That's not it."

"How about that one."

"Yes. That's him."

Taxidermist Bill Warren works in his Lansdowne workshop, where he's been 'mounting' wildlife for 16 years

A photo from *The Kingston Whig-Standard* showing taxidermist Bill Warren working in his shop.

"He looks good," I said, still staring at the deer that I had killed almost a year ago. "And he seems so alive," I added.

The word *taxidermy* comes from two Greek words: *taxis* meaning movement and *derma* meaning skin. The translation *movement of skin* seems appropriate, since part of taxidermy involves removing the skin, including the fur, feathers, or scales from the animal and pulling it over a moulded plastic manikin.

A taxidermist uses many skills such as woodworking, tanning, sculpting, painting, and drawing to apply the craft of trying to make a dead animal, dead bird, or dead fish appear lifelike.

Many people will be surprised to know that a taxidermist uses only the skin and antlers when mounting a white-tailed buck. The eyes are made of glass, the eyelids are sculpted from clay, the nose and lips are painted, the inside of the ears are airbrushed, and the manikin is carved from polyurethane foam. Some fish mounts are completely recreated from man-made materials and can be produced based on a good colour photo and measurements. In this case, a fish that was released live can still be mounted on the wall.

The preferred phrase in the business is *mounting the animal* as opposed to *stuffing the head*. The term stuffed animal comes from the nineteenth century. In those early days of taxidermy, upholstery shops stuffed animal skins with rags and cotton and sewed them up into crude-looking reproductions.

Taxidermy today has become a form of wildlife art, and taxidermists are full-fledged artists. Their creations are exhibited in museums, schools, clubs, businesses, restaurants, stores, and homes. They create realistic settings and artistic poses for all kinds of creatures from delicate little hummingbirds to full-sized elephants. Roy Rogers, the King of the Cowboys, had a full body mount made of his horse, Trigger, and his dog, Bullet. Both his animal companions are on display at the Roy Rogers/Dale Evans Museum in Branson, Missouri, which gets 200,000 visitors per year.

North American gamehead mounts of deer, moose, elk, caribou, bear, and mountain goats are among the most frequently mounted in taxidermy. The technology of mounting has progressed so quickly that award-winning gameheads from ten years ago wouldn't even receive honourable mention today. Tools and supplies have improved in quality and manikins are more lifelike because they are carved to include the fine details of tendons, muscles, and veins. A wide variety of urethane gameheads is available in various poses, sizes, ages, and seasonal variations, such as the swelled neck of a rutting buck. This ensures the best fit for the hide of an individual animal.

I had the first buck I shot mounted in 1986. He still hangs on the wall in my office at home and looks over my shoulder out the window while I write. When my daughter was young and before she could speak I would hold her in my arms in front of that head on the wall. Then I would point and say, "That's an eye," or "Those are the ears." One day when I said, "Where's the nose?" she lifted her arm and touched it with the tip of her finger. Eventually, she pointed and said, "ear" or "eye" or "nose."' Those words were among the first imprinted on her mind. It was important to me that she not only speak the words but also see a state of mind and a way of life.

The taxidermy process begins when the animal is skinned with a sharp knife to separate the hide from the flesh and bone. During skinning, the hide is slit down the back of the neck from the top of the head to the middle of the shoulders so it can be pulled easily over the manikin. Then the hide is dry salted and tanned or preserved with chemicals. Next, the eyes are set with clay and the antlers are screwed onto the plywood back of the foam head. The hide is pulled over the manikin and glued in place. Then the slit at the back is stitched tight to close and conceal it. The mount is then screwed to a finished wooden board and left to dry for approximately two months before the final touches are applied. Coloured waxes and sculpting compound are used to rebuild tissue and restore natural colour. The work is finally complete when the insides of the ears are airbrushed and the lips, nose, and eyes are touched up with oil paint.

Bill Warren, who hunted and fished and trapped as a boy, says his love of the outdoors made taxidermy a natural choice. He's made a career out of taxidermy for sixteen years. He mounts about forty deer heads a year. He also works on game fish like pike and pickerel in his 1,400-square-foot shop/showroom, which is heated by a wood stove. Any unused parts and scraps are returned to the woods where they are eaten by blue jays, foxes, and coyotes.

"Fishers love my leftovers," he told me with a smile.

Taxidermists exist because there is a demand for their art. It's important to ask why that demand exists. Why do some people want to mount the head of a dead animal on the wall? The answer is because it's a trophy. It's that simple.

A gamehead is not kept and displayed for social prestige like a trophy wife. A gamehead isn't attached to a ribbon and pinned to your chest like an engraved medal. It can't be worn on your head like a wolf-skin war bonnet or eagle-feather headdress. It's not paraded around stadiums or down crowded streets past cheering crowds like a silver cup. Nor is it held up high for adoring fans to see as if it were the severed head of some conquered king killed on the field of battle.

Instead, a trophy head is put in a place of honour. It is kept and displayed for the same reason that cave dwellers painted images of bison herds and wounded boars on the walls of their caves—because they were in awe of the power and beauty and spirit of the wild animals they hunted and killed.

I hung my trophy on the wall beside the only door of our hunting camp. The eight-point buck looks towards the woods where he lived and died. He comes alive each time I look at him.

I see his final drama unfold as it did that morning he raced down a distant ridge and crashed through the November woods towards the beaver dam where I waited and watched. When he tried to stop suddenly, he skidded out onto the open ground along the shoreline. Then his head made a quarter turn to the right as it does now on the wall. When he saw me, his big eyes bulged and he froze with fear. Only his final breath moved, drifting away from him and disappearing over the swamp.

Sometimes people require a little coaxing before they agree to let you write about them or put their story in a newspaper or book. They often become more agreeable if they feel there's something in it for them. I told the taxidermist that if he let me write about him and his craft I would give him a small bit of immortality—like the nameless, fearless, lifeless heads of the dead animals we put on our walls.

CHAPTER 16

One does not hunt in order to kill; on the contrary,
one kills in order to have hunted.

From Meditations on Hunting *by Jose Ortega y Gasset*

"I've done enough killing."

When someone recently told me that he had decided not to hunt anymore I was surprised. I wasn't surprised when he told me why.

"I've done enough killing," he said.

Killing is the reason that most people don't hunt. Killing is seldom why someone stops hunting.

The average hunter only kills one deer every three or four years. If killing were the goal of hunting, most hunters wouldn't hunt at all. Instead they would just go and buy a crate of chickens and beat them to death with a baseball bat. Killing them would be a lot quicker and much easier and far cheaper than hunting.

Some of my most memorable and enjoyable hunts were unsuccessful. But if you hunt, eventually you will be confronted with a chance to kill. If you want to keep calling yourself a hunter, sooner or later you will have to kill a wild animal.

No animal wants to die. Not a single factory farm animal would willingly give its life just so you can put a steak on the grill or wear leather shoes on your feet. Before condemning a hunter for killing, you must first justify being directly responsible for the deaths of thousands of animals that will be killed during your lifetime because you want to eat or wear them.

No factory farm animal escapes the slaughterhouse. Wild animals spend much of their lives avoiding death and danger. They are alert and elusive and tough. They are not tame and docile and fat like domestic animals. In the woods they are far more capable than the people who hunt them. That is the reason we hunt them.

A white-tailed buck is one of the most difficult big-game animals in the world to kill. I'm not referring to a park deer that stands around on a hiking trail and lets you take its picture, or a farm deer that grazes in an open field like a cow, or a city deer that thinks people are harmless. I'm talking about a swamp buck that lives a secret and solitary life of hardship while being pursued by coyotes and bears in the big woods and rocky ridges around the swampland it calls home.

In spite of the challenge and uncertainty of hunting, some people have become very good at it. But unlike other pastimes, if you become too good at hunting it can get to be like killing in a slaughterhouse.

Perhaps the man who told me "I've done enough killing" stopped hunting because he had reached that point. It's possible that he not only became a superb marksman, but a hunter who knew the woods and the habits of the animals living inside them.

Maybe he learned to respect life more as he got older. Growing old has a way of changing how people think. Perhaps he is one of those rare people who came to the realization that taking life for any reason is not justified. I can only guess.

Some hunters still get angry when they read in the newspaper the truth that hunting involves killing. Perhaps they have never confronted their conscience about why they kill. Maybe they don't want to justify and explain it to friends or family or to themselves. It's possible that they kill for the wrong reasons, like the great American writer Ernest Hemingway.

I respect Hemingway as a writer but not as a hunter. I've read most of his books and short stories on hunting. But when I read about his hunting trips I was shocked by the large number of big game animals he killed over a matter of weeks or days.

While on safari in Africa, he paid a large entourage of expert guides, trackers, gun handlers, skinners, porters, cooks, and personal aides to accompany and assist him. I don't consider it hunting when other people are paid to do all the preparing, planning, and pursuing and you go along to do little more than pull the trigger.

I think that Hemingway kept hunting just to prove his manhood. Perhaps he needed to. His mother dressed him up like a little girl when he was a young boy. I also thought it was fitting that when he pulled the trigger on his final shot, the barrel of the shotgun was in his mouth.

It's harsh criticism, but maybe Hemingway would never have fired that last fatal shot if he had said to himself, "I've done enough killing."

CHAPTER 17

A hunter in our camp had a beagle named Bear. He had brought the beagle deer hunting each year from the time it was born. But his family at home in the city became attached to Bear and only let him come to the hunting camp to get away and not to hunt. The man who owned Bear had to promise his family that he wouldn't take Bear into the woods with the other dogs in case something happened.

He was good on his word. Bear was like a pet dog around the camp. He even slept inside the camp stretched out by the fire or on one of the old couches.

During the Christmas holidays one year, some men went back to the camp to ice fish at a nearby lake. Before the cold weather arrives the camp is always winterized. The pipes are drained and clear light blue anti-freeze is poured in the toilet bowl so it doesn't freeze and crack.

As usual when everyone went fishing, Bear was left in the camp with a warm fire. The door to the bathroom was always shut so he wouldn't go in and drink the sweet-tasting but lethal anti-freeze in the toilet bowl. But this time the door wasn't closed tight. Bear managed to pry it open with his nose and paw.

When everyone got back, he was dead on the floor.

BLOOD, BULLETS, AND WORDS

Hunting always arouses strong feelings. People are either passionately for it or passionately against it. Over the years, my columns in *The Kingston Whig-Standard* about hunting have provoked many letters to the editor, most of them condemning hunting as blood sport and hunters as mass murderers.

Some readers attack hunting because they think hunting only means killing. Yet they never complain about the half-million factory farm animals that are put to death every hour of the day, in the United States alone, for meat and profit. Puritans condemn hunting not because animals are killed or suffer sometimes but because of the enjoyment it gives to those of us who hunt.

Writing about hunting has taught me that true friends can disagree and still be friends. Some people might be surprised yet pleased to learn that I have also found division and criticism within my hunting community, but for a different reason. When I arrived at the hunting camp one November, I was told I would be voted out of the camp if I wrote another hunting column that mentioned killing.

The hunters who threatened to vote me out were convinced that writing about killing jeopardized the future of hunting by upsetting people. I argued that ignoring such a basic truth would be like pretending it never happened and amounted to admitting that hunting was wrong. The ultimatum stood, but I refused to soften or bend my words.

It came down to the word "kill." Anti-hunters have always said, "Don't do it." Now, members of my own gang were saying, "Don't write it." I decided to resign rather than be censored. But there was someone who said: "Don't worry, I'll make sure you have a place to hunt next year."

He was an original member of The Terrible Ten. He remembered, as I did, that we were friends and how we became friends—through hockey, initially, and later while hunting.

Writing about hunting has helped me to know life and understand death. Killing is inseparable from hunting. We hunt expecting death. But giving and seeing death helps us understand dying and living.

Still, some hunters won't talk openly about the kill. They choose to continue to hide in the woods, so to speak, in the same way the gay community hid in the closet for such a long time. Yet hunting makes you more alive because you participate in, and begin to know, the natural world while hunting. In that world, death is always near, constantly avoided, and, for some hunters, finally understood. And to understand death is to understand your own insignificance.

Finding the writer in you

'One of the keys to good writing is to make the reader think that writing is easy'

LEY

BOUT MY DOG."
e about my business."
it my problem."
Whig-Standard published
nn in 1995 I've been asked
ut all kinds of subjects
rs. But there's one thing
want me to write about
e. I can't remember the
imes that someone has
the eye and said, "Write

e where I often eat, I al-
cook that she makes the
e ever had. One day she
write about her soup. A
e asked me if I'd finished
:olumn. I told her that I
on demand.
d. Maybe I should have
at she write it herself. I
ered to help by giving her
about writing a newspa-

possess the urge to ex-
ilves and to be creative.
vritten words as a means
. Few writers can get up
ing and write about the
hey see or think about.
bout things that inspire
o them. But something
aspiration and urge to sit
te. For me it's an idea.
idea just presents itself.
rom seeing something as
omeone feeding a duck
iterfront or from some-
ple as watching people
uugh a revolving door at
eral Hospital.
an idea hits you suddenly
the face. You look over

Picture in *The Kingston Whig-Standard* showing the author writing in his office with a white-tailed buck mounted on the wall behind him.
Photo courtesy of Michael Lea.

Writing about hunting has taught me to remember, and be grateful to, those responsible for the right to choose. For fourteen years, on the morning of November 11, I watched a man attach something to his hunting cap that is common tradition across Canada on Remembrance Day. But on that November day, as he pinned a blood-red poppy to the front of his blaze orange hunting cap, I thought: "He is only pretending to remember." More important, I realized that I was pretending, too. I admit that only then did I understand the importance of remembering that millions of young men and women poured out their blood and tears in two world wars so people would be free to think, speak, and write what they feel and believe.

Now I am free to write and to hunt, though many, if given the chance, would gladly take away my right to both.

Writing about hunting has taught me that nothing lasts forever. I will miss the old camp and The Terrible Ten. They were my teachers. They took the time to teach me about the rituals of hunting life and the rhythms of wildlife. In the darkness of the woods, they showed me how to find my way, where to wait and aim, when to shoot, and most important of all, when not to. In a fatherly way, they taught me secret things that few people will ever know, do, or feel. Such things are destined to slowly disappear, for these old ways can take a lifetime to understand.

The author in the woods with another member of the Terrible Ten loading two deer onto the front and back of a four-wheeler.

Though rich and sacred, they were tamed from the blood of most men long ago. Writing about hunting has taught me that hunting and writing share common ground. Being a predator is at the heart of both. To be successful at either, you must learn to watch patiently and listen carefully to the world around you and to yourself. One is as good as the other. Both require equal amounts of discipline, passion, bits of luck, and, above all, humility.

But in the moment of truth, everything is fair game only to the writer, who, if given the chance, could cover this page with blood, using only lead from a pencil.

CHAPTER 18

*People never lie so much as after a hunt, during a
war or before an election.*

Otto von Bismarck, first chancellor of the German Empire.

HUNT CLUB IN A HUNDRED-ACRE WOOD

Hunt Club meets Wednesday night during summer and fall. We
gather together at a place tucked away in a hundred-acre wood, which is
owned by a member's family and located along the shoreline of the
Cataraqui River just minutes from downtown Kingston.

Most of our time is spent cooking and eating while telling hunting
stories across a burning fire beneath the open sky. But we have also had
many exciting adventures in our forest.

We baited a black bear for months with a forty-five-gallon drum
filled with horse oats soaked in maple syrup. Nylon stockings stuffed
with chicken fat and skin were hung high in a tree over the drum to
draw the bear to the bait.

Another time we coaxed a white-tailed buck into an open meadow
by rattling two antlers together. The sound made him think that two
male deer had moved into his woods. Even worse, he thought they were
fighting for the right to mate with one of his does.

Hunt Club began in our hundred-acre wood when I let two friends
fire my high-powered rifle after obtaining their hunting licences. Three
memorable shots were fired that first night.

We tacked a target with an orange background and a white bull's
eye to a tree and paced off a hundred yards. In turn, Joe and Paul raised
the rifle and peered through the scope without the aid of a bench or
table or sandbags. While standing upright, they each squeezed the
trigger and hit the bull's eye on their first shot.

Then I tried. Before shooting, I had the presence of mind to say that I've never been known as a marksman. My shot missed the target and the tree. That became the first story of Hunt Club and has been told more times than I can remember, even by me.

Our hundred-acre wood has a large garden with row upon weedless row of eggplant, garlic, zucchini, tomatoes, and hot peppers that are picked when they turn red.

But our forest is not an enchanted one. The garden must be protected from the hunger of the inhabitants of the woods. It's been fenced in to keep the animals out. Anyone who has cared for a garden near a wild place knows that fences are not always enough.

Wild animals must be scared away with sounds and smells. White plastic bags tied to nearby trees and bushes flutter and flap in the wind and make a sound that is unsettling to wild animals because they rely on their ears to stay alive. Cuttings of human hair spread around the perimeter of a garden also provide protection, because the thing that a wild animal fears most is the scent of man.

The firepit is the centre of Hunt Club. It's where we form our circle to talk and cook and eat the wild meat that we kill ourselves. The meat is marinated in a mixture of brown sugar, soya sauce, vinegar, oil, onions, garlic, and ginger root for days ahead in anticipation of this night. Sometimes we eat so well that we joke and say, "Maybe Hunt Club should be renamed Diner's Club." But we eat all our food without knives or forks or plates.

Members of Hunt Club include two second-generation Italians, a Wolfe Islander, an Algonquin Indian, a man called "Neckshot," a hunter who grew up in the wilderness on the streets of downtown Toronto, and someone who has never hunted at all.

Upon arrival at Hunt Club, wood is cut, kindling is gathered, and the fire is started. We often sit at our fire wearing hunting boots, orange caps, camouflaged pants, and knives in sheaves on our hips. We sit on planks salvaged from an old homestead located on the edge of the hundred-acre wood.

As darkness descends around our fire, we can look across the river and see the Joyceville federal penitentiary. Each cell facing the river

Members of Hunt Club gathered at the firepit.

has a tiny window filled with light and the rows of lights can be seen from our fire. I sometimes wonder out loud what the prisoners in those cells think when they see our fire across the river every Wednesday night.

When the wood coals are glowing white, a series of cast-iron grills are taken down from a nail on a nearby tree. One grill became a topic of conversation at Hunt Club.

It was forged in the 1820s by the great-great-grandfather of one of the club's members. It is made of a thin flat metal ring sitting on three six-inch legs with small feet the size and shape of a quarter. The grill is placed in the hottest part of the fire and provides the foundation for the three grills that follow. A large rectangular grill is set over the circular one to provide a large cooking area. Two smaller square grills are then put over the rectangular grill so food won't be wasted by falling between the cracks.

The three-legged grill was brought to Canada from the "Old Country" in southern Italy. It came from the family farm in the province of Salerno near the town of Sassano. Even though it was scorched and twisted and rusted, it wasn't discarded or forgotten or left behind. That grill had survived the searing heat of countless fires and helped provide many meals both grand and humble, spanning three centuries, in the presence of innumerable friends, family members, and now Hunt Club.

When November arrives, the members of Hunt Club go their separate ways and travel to the northern woods, which are also the great woods because they are big and old and dark inside. We go to hunt the animals that we share our stories about while cooking and eating them at Hunt Club in the hundred-acre wood.

CHAPTER 19

Telling hunting stories is a common pastime in any camp, especially while sitting around the camp table after supper. In our camp, storytelling continues long after the lights are out and everyone is in bed.

I remember how everyone laughed in the dark the night I first told the story that became known as "the lion hunt." There were six of us lying in an army tent beside a beaver swamp.

I told everyone that if we won big in the lottery we should spend some of our winnings on a lion hunt. Hunting groups commonly buy lottery tickets together while deer or moose hunting.

"We'll hunt in two groups of three. Kenny, Francis, and I will hunt together," I said. Then I told them how we would hunt: "Kenny and I will sit in a blind, drinking and playing cards, and Francis will be fifty yards away tied to a tree.

"When he sees a lion he'll call out to us. Loud enough so we'll hear him in case we're preoccupied with the card game or sleeping, but not too loud in case he startles the lion. And he can't yell until the lion starts to charge."

When the laughter stopped, Francis said: "Do you hate me that much?"

"No," I replied. "I'm taking you lion hunting, aren't I?"

At night after everyone climbs in their bunks and the lights are turned off, something very unusual occurs at our hunting camp—something that I believe never happens in any other hunting camp in Canada. I read a bedtime story by flashlight to grown men until everyone falls asleep.

This ritual began years ago on a moose-hunting trip. One night while lying on our army cots in the tent and talking quietly in the dark, I raised my voice slightly and asked, "Does anyone want to hear a bedtime story?"

Today I tell a bedtime story every night whether we go to our camp to hunt, fish, work, or just to relax. But the ritual is always the same—everyone must be in bed and all lights must be off except my flashlight.

I tell one bedtime story per night in a small room with two windows and three sets of double bunks. I read from one of the top bunks in the corner while resting my back on a pillow propped up against the wall. I use a special headlight now. I fasten it to my head before climbing up my ladder in the dark. The light also lets me hold my book with both hands while reading.

My first bedtime story was one of the greatest survival stories of all time. It was about Ernest Shackleton's voyage of 1914 and how he led a frostbitten and starving crew of twenty-seven across 800 miles of ice and raging seas for months in a small lifeboat after his ship, *The Endurance,* was crushed by ice floes in the Antarctic.

One night I asked them if they wanted to hear the story of how Satan ended up in Hell. Then I told the tale of *Paradise Lost*, from the epic poem written by the blind poet John Milton. It's the story of man's first disobedience, the battle for Heaven, the creation of Hell, the temptation of Adam and Eve, the eating of the fruit from the Tree of Knowledge, and the loss of paradise.

Sometimes while telling a story like *Paradise Lost* I can't remember exactly what happened, what was said or by whom. So like any good storyteller I make it up as I go along.

Another night I started the bedtime story by saying, "I'm going to tell what may be the greatest story ever told, because storytellers have been telling this one for over 3,000 years."

Then I told the story of Homer's *Iliad,* which begins with a golden apple and ends with a wooden horse, and includes great warriors like Ajax, Achilles, and Hector, who fight for Helen of Troy, the woman with a face that launched a thousand ships.

Eventually I ran out of stories to tell. So one night I asked if I could bring a book and *read* the bedtime story. I asked, because you don't just bring a book to a hunting camp and start reading it out loud.

I knew the first story from a book had to be a good one, so I chose *To Build a Fire,* by Jack London, a story about man versus the wilderness. They liked it so much that I later read from *Call of the Wild* and *White Fang,* also by London.

I read for five-minute intervals. Then I stop and ask the same question every time, "Is anyone still awake?"

By then some people are already snoring but usually at least one person answers and says, "I'm still listening."

I've read bedtime stories by two famous American writers, Ernest Hemingway and William Faulkner. Not because they both won the Nobel Prize for literature, but because they wrote true stories about hunting and wild animals.

We usually discuss the bedtime story the next morning while preparing and eating breakfast. People recount what they remember and what they liked about the story.

Someone usually recalls at what part of the story he fell asleep. A person who stayed awake longer may say something like, "You missed the good part about how he panicked and froze to death after he couldn't start the fire."

Today, storytelling for adults is gradually disappearing, like the wild animals that inspired the first storytellers who hunted from caves where they lived. Sadly, the picture tube and the big screen have replaced the storyteller.

But every good story like those that I read at our hunting camp will live on forever, because those stories become a part of the people who hear them. They remain in your memory because as you listen you use your imagination to see the story. You feel the emotions and experience the adventures like the people in the story. From time to time you retell it to others and even to yourself. The story becomes real to you. It's as if you were in the story, too.

While sitting upright in the dark in my bunk, I keep reading until no one answers my question about being awake. Then I mark my page, put away my book, turn off my headlight, and go to sleep.

The bedtime story is over.

BOOK TWO
WILDLIFE

CHAPTER 1

The best-laid schemes o' mice an' men
Gang aft agley,
An' lea'e us nought but grief an' pain,
For promis'd joy!

Robert Burns, To a Mouse, On Turning Her up in
Her Nest with a Plough

"Wee, sleekit, cow'rin, tim'rous beastie"

Like the great Scottish poet Robert Burns, I once had a problem with a mouse.

In 1785, Burns wrote his famous poem entitled, "To a Mouse, On Turning Her up in Her Nest with a Plough." He felt sorry for the wee "beastie," whose nest he had overturned while ploughing his field. The mouse ran off in fear and Burns wrote about the incident in his Scottish dialect and language spoken by the common man:

Thou need na start awa' sae hasty
Wi' bickering brattle!
I wad be laith to rin an' chase thee
Wi' murd'ring pattle!

"Murdering" the mouse was the last thing on Burns's mind, but when I spotted one running across the carpet in my hallway, my first thought was to kill it.

I didn't have a mousetrap or poison or even a cat, but I knew of other ways to kill a mouse. Sitting alone in my kitchen, I recalled two particularly devious methods I had heard about.

I decided to try the water method. Like all living things, a mouse needs water. So I left a large pot half full of water in the middle of the kitchen and laid one end of a stick on the handle and the other on the floor. If the mouse were thirsty enough, it would crawl up the elevated runway to the rim of the pot and jump in. It won't think about how it's going to get out; and of course it can't. A small smear of peanut butter at the water line would be certain to help lure the mouse to its death.

After two days, there was no mouse in my pot.

I decided to buy some spring traps rather than try the other method. It's a variation of the first, only this time a piece of cheese instead of peanut butter is used for bait and placed at the bottom of a large and empty plastic pail. I remember asking the man who told me about all this, "How do you kill the mouse after it jumps into the pail?"

He replied, "I poke it with a ruler. Then it starts jumping, trying to escape. But it can't escape. The sides of the pail are too steep and smooth. So it just keeps jumping until it has a heart attack."

I asked if I could use his name. I was surprised when he said, "sure, go ahead." But I decided not to. I don't want people thinking my father is crazy.

Sometimes on the phone, I ask if he has caught any mice lately. He replies, "Dead or alive?"

I set out two of those standard surprise-your-neck-is-snapped mousetraps. They're like mechanical snakes; coiled and ready to strike, except they're deadlier because mice don't fear them like they do real snakes.

Have you ever seen what a store-bought feeder mouse does after being put in a glass cage with someone's pet snake? The mouse is so overcome by fear and panic that it repeatedly hurls itself against the glass trying to escape. I put one mechanical snake in the kitchen and another in the basement. A week passed and nothing happened.

I checked both traps daily. I remembered other mice. At the hunting camp, we set traps for mice then bet on which one would catch the first mouse. I've seen mice escape from traps by chewing off a leg or their tail. Some drag the trap away even with two broken hind legs. I even saw a double-kill once.

At the food store where I worked as a teenager, we caught mice in traps that looked like shoeboxes. When a mouse entered the open doorway in the front, a spring device was activated that pushed it into a separate, enclosed compartment in the back. A single trap often contained many mice before they were emptied in the toilet bowl, dead or alive. But mostly they were dead. Mice are wild animals and they did what you expect wild animals would do after being confined together for a long period in a small, dark, crowded space without food or water.

I kept looking around my house and in my cupboards but couldn't find any mouse droppings or crumbs of food anywhere. Mice are good at avoiding detection. Like most wild animals, their existence depends upon stealth. They build nests beneath floorboards and inside walls. They sleep and rest all day, then scrounge for food at night. It's a humble lifestyle. Most people don't allow mice to coexist inside their homes. Mice not only carry and spread disease, they also damage property by gnawing on wire, wood, or upholstery. They're notorious breeders, too.

But house mice have it easy compared to lab mice, which exist only to die for science and the benefit of people. Medical experiments are performed on lab mice. We hurt them and make them suffer so we can feel better and live longer. Then we put them to death humanely, if there is such a thing.

Maybe a lab mouse will save my life one day. It could happen. The truth is: we owe mice; just like we owe all animals, including those we eat for food or have for pets or put to work, and especially the unfortunate ones we keep in zoos just so we can take our children there to look at them up close. Few animals today remain beyond our dreaded reach and grasp.

But mice are survivors. In the end, they'll outlast us. They can survive in fields, like Burns's mouse, or in houses like mine. They can live with disease and keep breeding. They can take pain and withstand suffering. They don't rely on medical experiments or other animals. And if need be, when the time comes, they will even kill and eat each other to stay alive, like those mice in that shoebox trap used at the food store.

Three weeks passed and there was still no sign of any mouse. Eventually I just gave up hunting it because that's what I was doing. Maybe it went next door or outside and the neighbourhood cat got it. Maybe it was just passing by or scouting out new territory. Grudgingly, I picked up and cleaned up my traps. Then I put them away in a drawer.

But I'll be watching. If I ever see that mouse again, it's dead.

Robert Burns and I are more alike than you might think. He was a farmer before he became Scotland's national poet and most famous son. That means he'll always be a farmer first. That means he was no stranger to killing animals. And that means if he had found that mouse inside his house and not in his fields, he might never have written that poem.

CHAPTER 2

"Ever eat beaver?" he asked.

"No," I replied.

Then he said, "I caught one eating the feed around my duck blind last fall. I snuck up on him, shot him, cut off his hind legs, and ate 'em. They tasted just like prime rib."

THIS IS NOT A FAIRY TALE

It's a cold morning in mid-January. Five men set out on foot through the woods. Along the way, the first man suddenly stops and says something as he points to a track in the snow. He speaks softly, as men often do in the early morning darkness.

The snow on the ground is deep, and shaded by the darkness of trees. Many are bent or broken from the weight of the snow. Every now and then, as the men weave their trail, there is a sudden flop as a mass of snow slides from a branch.

Within the forest, snow castles and snow bridges are everywhere. The woods are like a magical mystical kingdom. But this is not a fairy tale. There is no happy ending.

Within a half hour, the men emerge from the woods at the edge of a beaver pond. It is the first of many ponds they will visit. Except for a mound not far from the opposite shore, it looks like a barren snow plain. The beavers are inside their lodge beneath the mound, below the snow and ice, protected by wood and mud that is frozen to the hardness of concrete.

There is no talking as the five men start across the pond towards the lodge. The men continue to walk in single file, the way animals travel. It provides safety in case of sudden trouble or danger.

The ice on the pond is a foot and a half thick, as is the snow above the ice. The sun has risen and glows red as it begins its daily journey across the sky. From inside the lodge, the beavers can feel and hear the approaching men.

Two of the men carry knapsacks. In one there are a dozen sticks of dynamite, and in the other, a battery and wire. The men are there to "take back the land."

The local cottage association told the men that it had a problem and asked for help. A nearby farmer said: "I know beavers. They're a pain. Kill them all."

The men had tried getting rid of the beavers once before. They pulled out all the dams by hand. But the beavers rebuilt them within days, doing only what comes naturally.

Then a trapper was sent in to set his lines. He said: "Prices are good right now, about sixty dollars a pelt." But he didn't solve the beaver problem, either.

Today will be different. The ice is the key. It provides access to the lodge. The lodge and dams will be destroyed. Without their lodge the beavers will freeze to death. When melt-off begins and the spring rain comes, there will be no dam to hold the water and no engineers to build a dam. By summer, new dams will be useless; there will be no water to hold.

The dynamite blast is sudden and swift. The lodge is blown a hundred feet in the air and to pieces. All that remains is a hole in the ice. If the beavers left before the lodge was blown up, the weather and the wolves would be waiting.

When it is over, someone says: "There was really no other way. It's just like having a house full of mice—we had to get rid of them."

CHAPTER 3

Yes, life was there! Inexplicable life,
Still wasted by inexorable death.
There had the stately stag his battle-field—
Dying for mastery among his hinds.

From Tecumseh *by Charles Mair (1838–1927)*

BATTLE FOR SURVIVAL

The small buck killed the big buck this time. He did it by driving one of his antler tines through the eye socket and into the brain of his opponent.

Although he won the battle, the small buck would also soon be dead. His death would be even more dramatic than that of the big buck. It would happen in a way that you could not possibly imagine. His dead rival would be responsible. Only Mother Nature could create such a cruel and unusual fate.

It was mid-November and the rut was at its peak. The two bucks were engaged in a struggle to determine who would have the right to mate. They fought to the death. They fought to see who would give life to the next generation. They fought not because they wanted to but because they had to. Wild animals are driven by instinct and controlled by a natural order over which they have no control. In this case, their bodies had an overwhelming urge to mate and they were both willing to die to satisfy that need.

As they fought, they lowered and smashed their heads together using their pointed antlers both as weapons and as shields to inflict and prevent injury. When the lethal blow was struck, the small buck tried to pull back and raise his head at the same time. As he did, the antlers and the lives and the deaths of the two deer became locked together as one. For the small buck, it was the beginning of a living nightmare.

Already exhausted from the fight, he thrashed and shook and even lifted the body of his dead foe from the ground while trying to free himself. Though he could not, he kept trying. The whole time, the small buck could not move about, or eat, or sleep, or rest, or see anything other than the bloodied face and the single dark protruding and still open eye of the dead deer that was inches away from his own two eyes.

Days may have passed; and long nights. The more he struggled, the more attention he attracted to himself. And he knew this. Because avoiding detection is what deer do best. It's how they stay alive.

The wilderness is always watching, especially from above. The wilderness is always listening even from far away. No matter which way the wind blows, other animals soon appear where there is an opportunity. And inside the wilderness, they don't just come to look.

The crows arrived first and waited patiently in the upper branches of the surrounding trees. They knew their chance would come. High above, turkey vultures wheeled their silent circles in the open sky. Maybe that's what attracted the coyotes. Eventually they found the two deer.

There were five coyotes. A pack. Even the coyotes had never seen anything like this. One remembered seeing a buck with his rack tangled in a barbed wire fence. For an instant, he could see the tufts of hair that remained behind in the wire long after the buck had gone. That's how the coyote learned that fences meant danger.

The small buck was alive and standing as the pack approached. His head was lowered to the ground from the dead weight of the other deer. Coyotes know little of mercy but in wild places like the woods surrounding the city of Kingston, they often provide a merciful end to the sick, weak, old, and helpless. But on this day they would not provide mercy to the small buck. It was the big buck they were interested in. He was the easier meal. They would eat him first.

The five coyotes began to feast on the hindquarters of the big buck. As the small buck pulled the big buck by the locked antlers, the coyotes tore away large chunks of rotting flesh from the back legs. The small buck dug his hooves into the cool damp earth trying to back away. He dragged the corpse of the other deer over rocks and under pine boughs and through the woods to the edge of a tag alder swamp as the coyotes followed behind devouring its entrails.

The weight of the load on the neck and shoulders of the small buck was gradually diminishing as the body of the big deer slowly disappeared. The big buck had now become the smaller of the two deer. Over half his body was gone. But the small buck still could not free himself. He was far too exhausted to lift and run off with what remained of the carcass.

Eventually the crows descended on the scene. They landed on the ground and began pecking at pieces of the big buck's flesh and guts and bits of bone and sinew that were strewn about and too small to be of interest to the coyotes.

The coyotes had eaten their way to within inches of the head of the small buck when a hunter heard the commotion from a distance. The crows and coyotes scattered when he came into sight. As he approached, the small buck slumped to the ground on all fours still locked to the remains of the other deer.

Mercy was provided. And the silent circles narrowed.

CHAPTER 4

. . . with the horse which you take across country,
over timber, which you control only through your ability
to keep the animal from realizing that actually you
cannot, that actually it is stronger.

William Faulkner, Absalom, Absalom!

IT LOOKS LIKE FREEDOM AND FEELS LIKE SEX

It was my first time and I tried to prepare myself by imagining how it would feel. Although it was scary, I knew enough not to be afraid. That would only ruin it.

Then I sat in the saddle. Right away, I knew I would have to make that horse run as fast as he could go. I found out later nothing could prepare me for that.

I would ride Scanner, a big brown quarter horse that weighed over half a ton. There was a woman, too. She rode Ed.

We started from her parents' farm. She had grown up there, riding horses, swimming in lakes, and walking down dirt roads. I could see the kind of childhood she'd had. It showed on her face whenever she smiled.

In the woods, we trotted along trails blazed by her father for the horses, and for the people who love riding them. She showed me how to ride like a mother might teach her little boy how to walk on his own two feet.

"Lean this way, keep your upper body still, roll your hips with the motion of the horse, hold the reins forward and up, apply pressure with your legs, and remember, horses move away from pressure," she said.

We rode down country roads lined with trees and houses and farms that were far apart and separated by long fencelines and open fields.

The sun had risen high and it beamed down from a clean sheet of clear blue sky. I wondered if she had ever been kissed on a horse.

There was a backward glance, and I saw another mother, and another horse, and then a little boy, smiling as he rode it, near the checkout counter in a grocery store somewhere in Toronto. I had forgotten about riding that mechanical horse.

As we continued riding, other horses appeared, standing, looking, and waiting to greet us with their heads on one side of a sagging, four-rail cedar fence and their bodies on the other. They had heard us approaching, or had been told we were coming by the wind that I could see moving through the trees.

But there were things that I could not see along those country roads, around farms and about horses that the woman with me could. There was another woman, one I had never met, planting flowers in front of her house near the roadside. She was old but seemed young and cheerful. We stopped the horses to talk to her and she surprised me when we were introduced. "I know you," she said, "from your columns in the newspaper." I was pleased and I thanked her for it.

"Okay," I said, "it's time. I want to ride all out, as fast as Scanner can go." And so we rode like that, four times.

Later, I began to search for the words to describe the feeling of riding fast on horseback. For weeks, the thought of riding that horse ran in my memory as I tried to find the right words. Eventually a single word came. It was a word whose meaning I knew but never truly understood: horsepower.

But that horse was no machine, for inside him was a heart pumping blood, and lungs drawing breath, and a mind driving four legs to do what they did best. Each time I leaned forward and whispered, "Come on, come on," he ran even faster. I could feel his spirit and see it, too, off to my left, there on the ground, where his shadow ran carrying mine, where his head held steady, where his hooves pounded, and his legs stretched out, as his tail streaked behind. What an animal.

After our ride, a vet came to the farm to care for a horse with a bad cut that bled from under her back leg. He found her jugular with his hand and stuck a needle in it. When the horse went down, a circle of people stood around watching as the vet stitched the wound. Someone made a pillow of straw under her head and covered her eyes. Even the other horses looked on with concern.

Before we left, we went into the barn and noticed a big brown rat lying on a sack of feed and dying a slow, painful death. He had been poisoned, and blood dripped from his mouth and nose.

I thought that I should kill him because he was suffering. But I looked at his yellow teeth and long rat tail and decided not to.

I regretted it later. He had lived out his life, secretly, in and around the barn, stealing food and doing what comes naturally. Nobody would miss him, or even care that he was gone. No one had ever loved him, not like the horses.

CHAPTER 5

About 1,300,000,000 chickens are killed worldwide each year for food.

That's a big number to comprehend or even to say out loud.

It means 5,000 chickens will lose their lives during the two minutes it takes to read this next story.

Another 5,000 more will be killed every two minutes thereafter, all day, every day, all year, every year, for as long as people like eating chickens.

That's a lot of killing.

RICHARD THE ROOSTER

When he crowed every morning before dawn, someone sleeping inside our camp always said, "I'm going to kill that rooster."

But no one did.

At first there were two roosters living in the woods behind our camp. But a predator like a fox or an owl killed one a few days after they were released to live on their own. We found its feathers and a dark stain on the ground near the back door.

The person who initially owned both roosters said they were waking him up too early every morning and that he wanted to get rid of them.

Someone suggested that the owner take them to our hunting camp where we would eat them. But he thought the owner would kill them first. Instead the owner just let them go behind our camp around Mitten Lake near Kaladar. It was mid-June.

From that day on, whenever someone went to the camp to fish or work or relax, that rooster came strutting out of the woods within minutes. We began feeding him right away. He ate everything from corn on the cob to fish guts along with insects and acorns that he found on his own. He would even peck a piece of popcorn from your hand but never let you get close enough to touch him.

It wasn't long before someone gave him a name. We called him Richard. Naming him was a big step towards having him as a pet and would make killing him difficult, if not impossible—although he didn't do himself any favours whenever he crapped all over our gas barbecue.

Richard fended for himself for weeks at a time until someone showed up at the camp for a visit. There's plenty of natural food around during most of the year. When a camp member bought a bag of rice for Richard, I knew we were becoming attached to him.

Richard was a survivor. Like all roosters, he seemed outwardly confident. He crowed all day long and liked flapping his wings, which looks like another form of crowing. A rooster is loyal to his flock, which may be what he thought we were. Roosters can also be aggressive and will attack anything that they think will harm their hens.

Richard seemed happy in his new surroundings. Besides crowing and clucking, he made a cooing dove-like sound whenever we fed him. While we worked outside he hung around scratching himself or digging a hole so he could sit and rest in the cool, dark earth. He always seemed to know where everyone was, especially when you got around behind him. Maybe that's why he lasted so long.

One day he suddenly and unexpectedly pecked a cigarette

Photo from *The Kingston Whig-Standard* showing Richard the rooster at the hunting camp.

out of someone's hand. I never turned my back on him after that, especially in the morning when he followed me back and forth to the outhouse located about fifty yards behind the camp. Those spurs located at the back of his legs can cause a very painful puncture wound.

No one knew where he went at night. We thought he might be staying in the doghouse or roosting on top of the kennel. Four of us went out one night with flashlights but couldn't find him roosting. He must have had a good spot for spending the night—somewhere safe from predators.

But a safe place to roost wouldn't keep him alive for long. Short days and cold nights were coming. Soon there would be no insects to eat or food on the ground to forage. Even if there were we knew he would freeze to death by Christmas unless a fox or owl got him.

We could have spared him from suffering a long, slow death. Someone from the camp could have volunteered to take him home to a nice warm place for the winter. Some people would even call that merciful.

Richard's problem was that he was not a wild animal. Maybe his ancestors once were. But he became domesticated. That means he couldn't survive on his own.

It appeared that there was only one right thing to do. After all, he was just one chicken, and if we decided to kill him we would eat him. In the end, he would be no different than any other chicken.

After reading the column that I wrote about Richard in *The Kingston Whig-Standard*, a lot of people asked me, "Whatever happened to the rooster that was living in the woods around your hunting camp?"

People wanted to know if we had found a new home for Richard, or if some wild animal had killed him like our other rooster, or if we had decided to shoot him because he started crowing at three o'clock in the morning.

One weekend when a few of us went to the camp, Richard didn't come strutting out of the woods to greet us like he always had in the past. We immediately thought he was dead.

But one of the members arrived a little later with some good news. He told us that a man named Calvin Parks approached him in the

Kaladar general store and said, "I read that story in the Kingston paper about your rooster and I've seen him wandering around the camp near the road while driving by."

Then he asked, "Is he a Barred Rock rooster?"

"Yes, he is," was the reply.

Then he said, "I'll take him if you want. I have thirty Barred Rock hens and no rooster."

"If you can catch him, he's yours," was the response.

Everyone at the camp was elated to hear the news about Richard.

"He probably thinks he's gone to heaven," someone said. "Thirty hens and one rooster—he won't have much time for crowing now."

"Hell, he's probably dead already," someone else said, laughing.

We had quite a discussion about whether Richard was better off all cooped up in a henhouse with thirty chickens or living a life of solitude alone in the woods.

"After all, isn't that why we like coming back to the camp—to get away from it all?" I asked.

Someone else added, "That's why we liked him so much—because he was a solitary creature and a lone survivor living out here in the wilderness on his own. You have to respect him for that. Now he's become just like any other chicken—hand fed, watered, and living with a roof over his head. He'll never be the same. I wouldn't be surprised if he wants to come back. He liked being alone."

Various times during our weekend at the camp I heard different people say that they kind of missed our rooster and they wondered how Richard was doing in his new home with all those chickens.

Later in the week after I got home, I decided to phone Calvin Parks and ask him about how he managed to catch Richard and how he was making out in his new surroundings.

I received a big surprise when I made that phone call.

Calvin's wife answered. When I identified myself and asked about Richard she said, "We haven't gone over to pick him up yet."

"What?" I asked, thinking the worst.

"We thought there was no rush. He's been on his own out there for months," she said.

We then had a nice chat about chickens and roosters and I thanked her for the information about Richard and said that he probably won't be there if you go to try and pick him up later.

It seemed obvious that Richard the rooster was dead. He hadn't been seen for over a week.

I shouldn't have been surprised. The big surprise was that he lasted so long out there in the woods by himself. The wilderness is always watching and listening. Richard really didn't have a chance against the hunger and cunning of wild animals like foxes, fishers, and owls.

Whatever killed that other rooster during the first few days that Richard and he were left to fend for themselves probably came back one night for another meal.

Richard's short time with us at the hunting camp probably were the best days he ever knew. We will certainly miss him. At least he could say that he lived free. Not many chickens can say that. A lot of *people* can't even make that claim, and many of them have lived a lot longer than that rooster.

Many people will be sad that he missed his chance to live with all those chickens. But to me that sounds like quite a chore—just one rooster, a confirmed bachelor, too—trying to keep thirty hens happy all the time.

Maybe he is better off dead.

CHAPTER 6

I was invited to a wedding where the bride and groom were vegans. Neither ate meat or animal by-products such as cheese, milk, or yogurt.

During the reception, the best man stood and asked for everyone's attention so he could tell us what was planned for the night. At the end of his little talk, he told us what we would be having for dinner and finished by saying, "The bride and groom wanted me to tell you that no animals died as a result of their wedding."

DE-BEAKED CHICKEN SOUP

Pretend this is you: You're packed into a subway car so crowded with strangers that you can hardly move. People begin to panic from being confined together too long. They start to push and shove. Some even attack and try to kill each other.

The subway car is stopped. You're trapped in the tunnel where you'll spend the rest of your life. When the door finally opens, someone is waiting with a knife and slits your throat. But it's still your lucky day. A lifetime of misery is finally over.

That's how factory-farm chickens live. The ones we eat. These chickens aren't raised in farmyards but live in cages inside factories. They aren't even called chickens. In the poultry business, they are known as "broilers" or "meat birds."

If these so-called chickens could utter a single word in protest, it would probably be: "Why?" The answer, also in a word, is "profit." It's the only reason they exist. All aspects of their lives are controlled to make them grow as fast as possible at the least cost. To increase productivity, their feed is laced with growth hormones and antibiotics. As a result, they gain weight so quickly their bones sometimes can't support their bodies and they become deformed. But there's no penalty for bad looks or posture. They can still drag their twisted feet and limbs to the feed trough and they can still gain weight. To ensure they don't kill each other and reduce profits, part of their beaks may be cut off at an early age.

I don't object to killing chickens for food or for profit. I lived near the village of Sydenham once, where I raised my own chickens. I bought them as baby chicks. I gave them a place to live that provided warmth and protection. I let them roam free from time to time. I gave them food and water. Then I cut their heads off, one by one. And just so you know, they do run around without their heads, spurting blood out the hole at the end of their necks.

For months they ignored me. They didn't feel I was a threat—until the morning I walked into the coop with a hatchet in my hand. As my eyes fixed on the plumpest hen, I still remember how every chicken in the coop moved away, like the parting of the Red Sea. They knew which one I wanted.

Factory chickens are another matter. I object to the conditions they live under and the suffering they are forced to endure. A chicken, like most animals, will flee from danger or stand and fight. It's wrong to stereotype chickens as cowards. Anyone who has raised a rooster can attest to that. And mother chickens are just as caring and protective of their young as are other animals or people.

Chickens have evolved to establish a social pecking order, search and scratch for food, roost at nightfall, and crow at daybreak. While in captivity at the factory-farm, they are deprived of these natural habits. The more comfortable and normal we make their living conditions, the more expensive the cost per pound of chicken meat.

The chicken you find on the meat aisle of the grocery store is as natural as the cellophane and Styrofoam™ it's wrapped in.

In a hunting camp somewhere up the Spanish River, a Frenchman named Yvon—whom we all called Ivan—told me how he swung a sledgehammer for a living when slaughterhouses still killed by brute force, and how he could never wash that smell of misery, suffering, and terror off his body, and that he could still remember and smell it.

Factory farm chickens don't just smell it; they feel it, think it, and breathe it. I wonder what happens to our bodies when we eat their bodies? Depending on how much we eat, it could affect our health.

Like alcoholics who are consumed by the contents of the bottles they drink from, people who eat the living nightmare contained in chicken meat lose a small piece of their souls with each bite.

CHAPTER 7

The sledgehammer that my moose-hunting partner swung in the slaughterhouse had a long spike protruding from the end.

The cows he killed walked in single file through a wooden chute. When a cow reached the end of the chute, its neck and head hung out over a closed gate. A bar was slid across from behind and the cow became trapped in a small death stall.

Then someone slipped one end of a rope around the cow's neck like a noose and tightened it. The other end of the rope was passed down through a thick metal ring bolted to the floor directly beneath the cow's head. The rope was pulled tight so the cow was forced to lower its head.

When the cow's head was down, a man stepped forward and swung a sledgehammer like a baseball bat driving the spike into the cow's head. The force from the blow was concentrated at the point of the spike so it punctured the skull and pierced the brain.

Sometimes a second or even a third blow was needed. Between blows, a cow would moo in agony and kick the walls of the pen in desperation.

The other cows waited their turn. No cow escaped.

BULLHEADIN' IN SHAKESPEARE'S "UNDISCOVERED COUNTRY"

They all struggle. But not for long. They all die. But not right away. We kill them hours later, one by one, and they never make a sound. After all these years, the way it happens is beginning to bother me.

I'm still amazed at how they let themselves be caught. They are not aware of the danger until it's too late. No hook or net is needed. Maybe that's why it's called "bullheadin'" instead of fishing.

Bullheads are bottom feeders, about a foot long, black on top with white bellies. They're shark-shaped and have no scales. They have long whiskers beside their mouths. Sharp, horn-like barbs on the sides of their heads give them their name. Even when we fry them in butter and oil, they still taste a little swampy.

We catch bullheads with a "worm bob" that is tied to the notched end of a broom handle. To make a bob, a needle with fishing line is passed through the length of the bodies of about fifty worms until they're sewn together into a writhing ball.

But what happens to the bullheads after we catch them is much worse than what we do to the worms.

We bullhead during the night with lanterns, from an anchored pontoon boat. The first bullhead hits the bob within fifteen minutes after detecting the worms by smell. There is a tug on the line and, most times, the bullhead won't let go even as the line and bob are lifted slowly from the water and swung over a plastic barrel tied to the side of the boat.

Except for the hiss and glow of the lanterns, the lake and night are silent and dark.

The talk flows along. It's relaxed, almost sleepy. Even catching the fish is somewhat effortless. The middle of a lake, late at night, is a combination of place and time that gives a sense of the universe. I never let that night go by without saying: "For every hour you fish, you add an hour to your life." Who knows, maybe it's true.

Bob Stinson tells us of catching bullheads when he was a boy back in the '50s: "My grandfather was a milk inspector. He would stay with us whenever he passed through this area. He'd call ahead and my brothers and I would grab our poles and go catch a half-dozen bullheads for supper. He'd eat the bullheads and we'd eat the partridge he'd shot driving the back roads along the way. What I remember the most was he would always leave a $2 bill under his plate." This prompted his brother, Harry, to say: "Now there aren't any $2 bills."

Hunger is the reason bullheads attack the worm bob. Instinct is why they hang on. They become excited when they catch the prey. But they remain unalarmed because the lifting of the line feels like their prey is trying to get away. By the time they're in the air over the barrel, they sense the sudden change. But by then, it's over. The deception is complete.

When a bullhead finally lets go of the worm bob, it falls on the bullheads already in the barrel. It begins to struggle as they did. The others just lie there motionless. They are waiting, conserving their energy and making their lives last as long as possible. I grab a flashlight and look in the barrel. One tail thrashes and a single body twists, flopping across other bodies while slithering around the inside wall of the pail.

Later that night, I become inspired by the sight of the stars in the sky and the glimmer of their reflection on the lake. I smell the tall pines around the shoreline and hear a whippoorwill calling its name; I hear the screech of a nighthawk. So I recite a few lines of poetry. But first I tell everyone on the boat that I'm going to recite the lines and that they're by William Shakespeare and about death.

No one laughs. Everyone listens. I deliberately speak low so they have to. I want to say that death is "the undiscovered country from whose bourn no traveller returns."

Even though it's only two lines, I butcher them, but no one knows. Then I begin to think about all those bullheads in the barrel and how we're going to butcher them, too. Most have white bellies. But I know there will also be a few with yellow bellies. What happens to them is a fate worse than any other living creature I know of, except maybe a lobster.

We sometimes catch more than a hundred bullheads during a night. We kill them the following morning. We sleep first and have breakfast so we're well rested and full when we do it. The bullheads spend the night in the plastic barrel inside the hunting camp so the raccoons don't get them. We set up chairs and empty plastic pails around the barrel.

Harry and the author cleaning bullheads at the hunting camp.

A long, thin, sharp knife is used to cut a slit across their backs, directly behind the fin. When the knife goes in, their bodies vibrate and convulse in your hand. They are still alive and conscious. Two fingers from each hand are inserted into the slit on the back and the bullhead is ripped in two. When it's torn apart, one hand holds the pink, meaty flesh attached to the backbone and tail, and the other holds the head, still connected to the entrails, and eggs, if it's a female.

I contemplate another death scene near our little circle of chairs. We sit just feet away from a pinecone on a large flat rock near the shadows. The pinecone is half eaten and its seeds lie scattered in the sunlight on the rock. A red tail is all that remains of the red squirrel that died eating the pinecone. The red squirrel did not see or hear what had seen or heard it gnawing on the pinecone. The pinecone killed the red squirrel.

The red squirrel was being cleaned on the rock by something that eats flesh when a sound or movement frightened it away.

The bullhead flesh goes into one pail and the heads and guts into another. When bullheads are cleaned on a boat, there is no gut bucket. Sometimes the head and guts swim away after being thrown overboard.

We talk while sitting and cleaning the bullheads. When the man beside me tears one apart with his hands, I ask him if there is anyone he knows whom he'd like to do that to. He looks up from the barrel as he bends, reaching for another bullhead, and he smiles as he does it, while saying: "Oh yeah."

"We all have someone like that," I reply. He just smiles back at me.

Eventually I grab a bullhead with a yellow belly from the barrel. I throw it into the gut bucket, where it is slowly suffocated by the entrails of the other bullheads. I ask, but no one knows, why we don't clean and eat the bullheads with the yellow bellies. But I know the reason. It's because their skin is yellow and not white.

The next morning, a turkey vulture is standing beside the gut bucket with his red featherless head reaching inside. Two crows perched in a tree await their turn. Eventually we carry the gut bucket away and empty it into the creek behind the camp.

The bleached bones of the bullheads with the yellow bellies that were dumped the year before are still on the ground beside the creek, where they were dragged up from the water and eaten by scavengers and predators.

CHAPTER 8

I was trying to learn to write, commencing with the simple things, and one of the simplest things of all and the most fundamental is violent death. It has none of the complications of death by disease, or so-called natural death, or the death of a friend or someone you have loved or have hated, but it is death nevertheless, one of the subjects that a man may write of.

Ernest Hemingway, Death in the Afternoon

TURKEY VULTURES RIDE ON NATURE'S GRAVY TRAIN

I saw turkey vultures feeding. They looked filthy and hellish. I was on a hunting watch, crouched beneath a stand of pines overlooking the corner of an old unkept hayfield.

A pair of blue jays had arrived before me and took turns flying down from a tree to the gut pile of a four-point buck. The previous afternoon, we had dragged the dead deer across the field and taken it away in the back of a pickup truck. The jays struck the pile with their bills, then returned to their perch to swallow their meal.

The turkey vultures arrived later that morning. They circled low, as their shadows passed over the field beneath them. One by one, they glided down and began to run before waddling slowly over to join the feast. Five vultures squatted around it and went to work. From the safety of the tree, the jays protested loudly, crying, "Thief, thief!"

The vultures didn't see me. But like all wild creatures, they were watching even as they fed. Their eyes did the looking from small, featherless red heads sunk in dark, hunched bodies. I was close enough to hear them hissing and grunting as they tore at their food.

The bare head, face, and neck are unique features designed to keep the birds clean while poking around inside the body cavity of an animal carcass.

When the pile was reduced to a wet spot on the ground, the vultures left. They took off by running, then jumping, before lifting themselves slowly away on wings stretching six feet across.

It's either a curse to live a life that feeds on death or a free and easy ride on the gravy train.

Turkey vultures eat almost anything, but the tenderized remains of rotting animals are their specialty. They can't kill live prey because their claws are not designed for grasping and their hooked beaks are not strong enough to tear the hide of an animal. No one knows how they manage to digest diseased and contaminated carcasses without becoming ill or dying. They clean up a carcass quickly, convert it to fertilizer, and spread it across the countryside. If threatened, they regurgitate their last meal to startle and divert an attacker so the vulture can flee. The stench alone from such a ghastly shower, I'm sure, would sicken and stagger a goat.

Sightings of vultures on the ground are uncommon. Usually their dark, broad, V-shaped wings can be seen gliding gracefully high above the ground on thermal currents generated by rising heat. They soar above farmland, woodland, and roadways in search of their food. But what brings them down to the carrion below, from heights as far up as a mile? Do they smell it or see it? Probably both. Amazingly, they have been known to detect a hidden or covered corpse, the way they found the hunting dog Thunder buried in a shallow grave.

Roadkill is a major food source. Although common on country roads, roadkill is rarely considered obnoxious, because it's seldom seen, thanks to the turkey vulture. Cities have roadkill but no big birds. As a result, animal remains can lie around for weeks, crushed beyond recognition except for feet and wings that weren't fast when they needed to be.

I remember a night, long ago, when I learned how turkey vultures got their name. We were sitting around the hunting camp, talking about the big bird, how it looked and lived and what it ate. It seemed like a good question, so I asked: "Why are they called turkey vultures?"

The answer was quick and delivered in a tone implying that I was a turkey for even asking: "Because they have a red head like a turkey."

**A turkey vulture in a birch tree—the red head gives
turkey vultures their name.**
Photo courtesy of Alex Hudel.

CHAPTER 9

Smoke-blue he is, and grey
As embers of yesterday.

T.G. Roberts 1877–1953

DEATH THE IMPALER

Early one morning, I was surprised to see a great blue heron while walking to work. He was down among the rocks and driftwood along the shoreline of the La Salle Causeway, looking not like a heron but a thinly disguised, ghostly apparition of one. I was on a bridge less than twenty yards away. Most herons usually fly away long before you get that close. Perhaps he didn't think I had seen him. He stood still and looked proud and reminded me of a statue of grey stone in a city square.

The stillness of the great blue heron is a moving sight. Spotting him, alone and motionless, gave me a feeling of awe and quiet comfort, as if nature has rewarded me for paying attention to what is really there. For every one I have seen in the wild, I know there were ten or more I didn't see, laced in sunlight or veiled in shadow, standing half-hidden among the bending reeds, or waiting like a phantom, there in the shallows, or behind the twisted skeleton of some dead and fallen tree.

If you look closely you may see his yellow eyes move slowly like searchlights. Able to focus independently, they survey his surroundings, watching for danger above and carelessness below. If he tolerates your presence, which is rare, and if you're patient, you may see him move, gracefully lifting his long legs through knee-deep water. But you will never hear the stealthy footsteps of his dark, deliberate feet as he stalks his prey.

Eventually the heron at the bridge flew away. As he lifted off, angling away, rising above the water, he became suddenly beautiful and strangely elegant. His thin legs trailed behind, stiff and straight, as his six-foot wings beat, slowly, powerfully, and gracefully.

A great blue heron is more than four feet tall but, incredibly, weighs less than ten pounds. His long, slender body seems frail and faded. He looks vulnerable, but he's not. He is a survivor who has been around for sixty million years, a living dinosaur, like the great white shark and the saltwater crocodile. To those he silently stalks, he is Death the Impaler.

Wise and patient, he lurks in the empty waiting rooms of shorelines, marshes, and meadows, watching for a frog, fish, or some other small creature to happen by and wander in, unwary and unconscious of its fate. He is a regular visitor to these quiet, peaceful, graveyard places. He strikes with blinding speed, like a snake. His yellow, rapier-like beak is six inches long and tapers to a sharp point.

He doesn't actually catch his prey. He sets himself, eyes, neck, and legs together, then runs his victim through near the head, using his beak like a spear. Then he opens his beak a bit to keep the prey from sliding off. He must compensate for the bending of light through water, striking where his brain, not his eyes, tell him. Once speared, anything unlucky enough to be alive after the first strike is carried away, and beaten or stabbed to death, usually against a rock. Like many deadly predators, he hunts alone, by day or night.

Pesticides and loss of habitat have diminished heron numbers, but humans have little or nothing to fear from them. A word of warning, though: don't get too close to an injured heron; he can take your eye out.

When I stopped to look that morning, the heron gave me this story, and with it an unpleasant, forgotten memory of another great blue heron I had seen on another morning long ago.

I was in a duck blind, but no ducks came, just a solitary heron flying over a beaver pond. He passed by, low and broadside, just above the morning mist. He turned his head and seemed surprised to see me there. It was so quiet I heard the unmistakable creaking of his long, broad wings. That sound faded from my hearing as he disappeared from sight.

Then there was a shot and a splash. We were not alone. Someone else was there in the swamp that day. I wonder if he remembers what happened, or if he ever thinks about that great blue heron.

CHAPTER 10

When I was twenty-three, I moved to the countryside north of Kingston from downtown Toronto. In the big city, I had been an accountant with a multinational corporation called Alcan. I earned a big salary, wore three-piece suits, and worked in a glass office with carpeted floors on the thirty-fourth floor of a big black tower called the Toronto-Dominion Centre.

One of my first memories of living in the country was of all the dead animals I would see along the road while driving back and forth to work in Kingston. Often I would get out of my car for a closer look at a dead fox, porcupine, or raccoon. I'd linger over them, admiring their teeth and claws and fur. People I knew would see me by the roadside and I became the butt of endless jokes about my interest in roadkill.

I'll never forget the first time I saw a cow up close. I was going to a pig roast one Saturday in a friend's pickup truck. When we turned down a gravel road near Loughborough Lake, there was a herd of cows standing along the fence line in the shade of some trees. I asked my friend if he would stop so I could take a closer look. Laughing, he warned, "Watch out they don't bite."

He pulled two beers out of the cooler in the back of his truck and joined me at the fence. As I got closer, I said, "My God, look at those cows."

"What about them?" Peter replied, surprised. He looked at the cows to see if there was something unusual he had missed.

"They're all covered with hair," I said, totally amazed.

"What did you expect?" he asked.

"I thought they had leather skin, like a coat or a football."

The duck approached not as you would expect, by water or in the air. Instead, it walked down the length of the wooden dock up to our boat. It quacked, attracting attention to itself as it waddled towards us. Even its "quack, quack, quack" sounded odd. It wasn't a warning, but more like a greeting. It seemed to be asking, "Got any food, got any food?"

We were sitting in a boat moored along the Kingston waterfront. Our captain and host that day knew the duck. He didn't call it by name. But he spoke to it in a soft, reassuring voice the way someone would speak to his or her companion animal. "Hello. Wait there. I've got something for you," he said.

He leaned from the boat and reached out with his hand to offer the duck a piece of bread. When the duck stretched out her neck to grab it, she slipped from the edge of the dock and accidentally hit her head on the wooden diving platform at the stern of the boat. Then she flopped sideways into the water with a splash. She seemed to squawk with disapproval because her feathers and bread had gotten wet.

Within minutes, from out of nowhere, her nine ducklings appeared, along with another family of ducks and numerous ring-billed gulls, which began dive-bombing the boat for bread.

The man feeding the ducks said: "They like me. Sometimes I feed them Pringles potato chips right out of my mouth."

The scene is a familiar one along the Kingston waterfront, especially at Confederation Park in front of City Hall. During the summer months, tourists and local people walk along the shoreline and feed the ducks. They often bring young children who delight at seeing ducks and gulls up close when they approach for food.

While sitting on a bench at Confederation Park, I coaxed a duck so close to me that I was able to knock it with my foot. I didn't even have a piece of bread in my hand. I just dangled a paper wrapper near the ground in front of the duck.

I've seen a lot of wild ducks over the years, occasionally while looking down the barrel of a gun but more often through binoculars. In the wild, the instant a duck sees a human being, it tries to get as far away as fast as possible. If a wild duck sees you coming, it will fly away before you get within two hundred yards.

That's what makes an animal wild: its fear of people. And if you take away an animal's wildness, you take away its life.

Wild ducks have been dispossessed of their wildness by people who feed them. They become city ducks: dependent on handouts and comfortable around people even to the point of aggression. While walking to work during the winter months, I've seen what happens to city ducks when the people who feed them stay home. They starve or freeze to death. Their bodies are frozen in the ice along the LaSalle Causeway.

Maybe the city should put up a warning sign about not feeding the ducks. Ducks in the wild eat aquatic plants, insects, fish, berries, acorns, and grain. The ingredients of potato chips include monoglycerides, maltodextrin, acetic acid, malic acid, and sodium acetate.

People who feed bread, potato chips, and donuts to ducks either don't know or don't care that they're harming—not helping—them. We feed wild ducks for one reason—the same reason we keep wild animals in the zoo and exploit them in the circus and bait them in the wilderness—for our own pleasure.

A real animal lover wouldn't feed a wild animal, not at Confederation Park, not at the zoo, not in the backyard, not in the wilderness, not anywhere.

CHAPTER 11

Love the animals. God has given them the rudiments of thought and joy untroubled. Don't trouble it, don't harass them, don't deprive them of their happiness, don't work against God's intent.

Fyodor Dostoevsky, The Brothers Karamazov.

"HE WHO SITS IN THE SHADOW OF HIS TAIL"

Rain frightened him, so when the downpour ended, he was bright-eyed and bushy-tailed. Starting out that morning, he was travelling on his usual route from his home in the attic to a neighbourhood bird feeder. Leaping across the cedar fence line, he looked down and saw the open cage.

The cage was carefully placed on the ground behind the shed, where it couldn't be seen from the windows that overlooked the yards. The sunflower seeds inside the cage made him stop. Never having seen a cage, he approached cautiously, coaxed eventually by hunger beyond the threshold of fear.

Squirrels are among the animals that have learned to coexist with humans. As woodland and natural habitat are cleared and developed, displaced squirrels have successfully relocated to urban areas in search of new homes and food sources.

Their natural predators have disappeared either because they did not adapt or they were systematically eliminated due to some real or perceived threat to people. As a result, squirrels flourish in the city. Like many urban animals, they cross our streets, prowl our yards, eat our precious plants, and even live in our houses. For some people, they have moved too close to home.

The sunflower seeds in the trap were the squirrel's last meal. During that first outrageous day in captivity, he gnawed continuously on the metal bars, stopping only to voice his displeasure by tchrring in a high-pitched shrill call.

Squirrels are rodents that take their name from the Greek word *sciouros*, meaning "he who sits in the shadow of his tail." A squirrel's tail is used for balance when climbing, as a rudder when leaping, and as a means of communication. It also provides warmth. Flicking is the most common tail gesture. It means "get lost." That wonderful tail makes the squirrel one of the most recognized mammals on earth.

The next day, the steel cage preyed on the squirrel. The bars imprisoned him until his body was limp and his spirit broken. He gave up trying to find the opening that was there when he entered the cage. He spent his time curled up inside his tail.

Squirrels live about six years, except in the city. Most urban squirrels don't live to see their first birthday. This is due not to the triple onslaught of traps, guns, and poison, but to an invention just over a hundred years old: the automobile.

The homeowner was away that weekend. When he finally checked the cage, the squirrel was in shock. He had begun to tear out patches of his own fur, driven by the nesting instinct.

The squirrel is the result of fifty million years of evolution and is fast for his size, dashing up to twenty miles per hour. When facing a speeding car, a squirrel runs erratically across its path, attempting to confuse and cause the car to change direction. Still, he cannot escape the wheels of progress speeding towards him.

Under cover of night, the cage was taken away, towards the house. There was a short-lived glimmer of hope as the squirrel's gaze slipped past the metal bars towards the approaching rain barrel and a tiny, hidden hole high above it, the doorway to its attic home.

The urban squirrel is a tightrope walker in nature's balancing act. Daring and free-spirited, he lives on the edge. He can leap up to six feet, on the ground or through the treetops. Few bird feeders are beyond the reach of the acrobatic squirrel. His survival depends on hiding and burying food. The squirrel licks it, depositing his scent, thus helping him find the food later, even under a foot of snow.

Like his street-smart brother, the sewer rat, the squirrel's incisor teeth grow continuously throughout his lifetime. He chews on tree branches and wires to sharpen and clean them. He urinates to mark his territory, warning other squirrels not to trespass. In adulthood, he lives alone. But, during periods of severe cold, he will share a nest to conserve body heat and stay alive.

There was a time when the man who owned the cage released the squirrels in a wooded area behind the hockey arena by the river instead of taking them to the rain barrel. Then one day, a man walking a dog along the riverbank confronted him: "Take your problem somewhere else. You people from town all bring your damn squirrels out here. They're everywhere. I trapped almost fifty last year myself."

"What do you do with them?"

"That's my bloody business."

CHAPTER 12

Coyotes were killing more sheep and calves and pets than usual. The ministry agreed to come and speak to local farmers and cottagers and people living on rural routes. They gathered at the Lions Club to discuss a proposal to put a bounty on coyotes again.

A couple who had recently retired and moved to their cottage also attended the meeting. They had lived and worked all their lives in Toronto. It was the woman who rose and spoke that night. She said she had been a teacher, too.

She told everyone she had a solution to the problem. She said, "Bait and catch the coyotes in cages and then neuter and release them again."

When she finished speaking, the room erupted with laughter when a voice from the back of the room boomed out, "They're not fucking them, lady. They're killing them."

WATCHING WILD ANIMALS

It was dark and late and early June. I was trying to sleep beneath the open sky on a blue mat on a large rock overlooking a long, narrow strip of land running between two swamps.

Three things combined to annoy me that night. The rock was uncomfortable. My sleeping bag was too hot to sleep in. And the mosquitoes wanted blood. Discomfort is often an unwanted companion inside the wild. But there are rewards, too. Mine came with the dawn.

The woods and swamps around the rock perch are hard to reach and difficult to find. There are no roads or waterways to take you to it. Few people go there. That makes it a haven for wildlife.

Watching animals in the wild can completely transfix and absorb you. It can make you forget time and that you even exist.

Four wild animals appeared at various times that morning. They were part of the drama we would witness from the rock.

We were watching a large snapping turtle basking on a stump when we spotted two does walking along the well-worn game trail on the strip of land between the swamps. The deer were forty yards away and moving from our right to our left. We had not seen them emerge from the lush green foliage. As is often the case with deer, they were suddenly just there, seemingly appearing from nowhere.

Both deer soon disappeared off to our left. One deer returned and walked a short distance into the swamp, feeding as she went, and stopping only when the swamp reached the top of her legs. Then a third deer appeared. It was standing on the shoreline where we had first noticed the other two.

Deer standing on the shoreline with its reflection in the water.
Photo courtesy of Steve Lukits.

It was a doe. Like us, it was watching the deer in the water.

The snapping turtle on the stump slipped into the shallow water and swam off hardly making a ripple. Its powerful strokes were graceful. Its dark shape, moving beneath the water, could have been mistaken for a shadow on the surface of the pond made by some great bird floating by overhead.

Suddenly the deer on the shore froze. Only its ears moved. First one, then the other, searched for sounds behind it while the deer stared straight ahead. The deer in the water immediately saw the rigid body language of the deer on the shore. So it stood perfectly still, its eyes locked onto the deer on the shore as if waiting for a cue to move again.

"There's something wrong," I whispered. "Something is going to happen."

That's when a third deer exploded out of the woods, trying with one great leap to jump from the strip of land across the swamp to the shoreline below our rock. It came up short.

Its large splash sent two other "white flags" up as the deer in the water and the one on the far shoreline bounded off in the same direction with their tails waving high. The first deer went by so fast that it seemed to be flying through the woods on wings like a bird in flight. Its body was elongated with speed while its feet and legs appeared not to touch the ground.

I remembered seeing another deer leap through the air into the water like that. It was in an obvious state of panic because of the black bear that leaped into the water a few seconds behind it. They were running a race, one that people rarely see. It's a race most people know little or nothing about. It's a race wild animals run every day. It's a race between fear and hunger.

When all the commotion stopped, I whispered again. "Something else is coming. Get ready."

Often heard but seldom seen, with his head steady, eyes ahead, and ears cocked, the predator at the top of the local food chain appeared. It was a coyote. He seemed to have given up the chase and was loping along the game trail. His body was lean and supple and his head and feet were thick and large. Unhurried, he passed by and stopped twice. He had paused to look in our direction after he came out of the woods. When he stopped the second time, he turned slightly and looked up and across the pond directly at us sitting on the rock. Then he was gone.

I never wear a watch. But my friend, who does, told me later that from the sighting of the first deer to watching the coyote disappear had taken nineteen minutes. That's a long time to watch animals in the wild. Yet the experience seemed to last only seconds, and now feels timeless.

BOOK THREE
THE WILDERNESS

CHAPTER 1

We are the stars that sing,
We sing with our light,
We are the birds of fire
We fly over the sky.

From an Algonquian poem

WE HAVE A PLACE

On a Friday in midwinter, a group from the office was going out for drinks after work. I brought a change of clothes with me in the car that day. But I wasn't going with them. Around six o'clock, I would be entering the wilderness north of Kingston to spend the night in the woods under the stars with a friend.

As we prepared to leave, his wife asked, "In case something happens, where will you be staying?"

I smiled and said, "What difference does it make? If they have to come looking for us, we'll probably be dead by the time they get there."

We started in the dark carrying our food and gear on our backs. Our destination was two hours away by foot. We followed the swamps and lakes, using them as winter runways like the animals do. Starlight reflecting off the snow lit our way.

As we started across the first swamp, we stopped. A beaver channel that ran through it resembled an unshovelled city sidewalk. "Stay to the left," my friend said; "there could be thin ice or open water beneath the snow of that channel."

As I lifted my left foot, my right one plunged through the ice up to my knee. I used the stick I was carrying to stop from falling forward and all the way in. For the next half hour, my foot squished with each step, but my body heat kept the swamp water warm inside my boot.

We stopped again before crossing a lake and I changed into one of my spare socks. Steam from my naked foot rose into the air as I pulled off my wet sock, which soon hardened in the iron night. I placed a green garbage bag over the fresh, dry sock and tucked the plastic under my wet pant leg and long underwear before putting my boot back on. I wore that bag for the remainder of our adventure.

As we stepped onto the next lake, a pack of coyotes howled. "That howl was for us," I said. "Those coyotes are close and they know we're here." Then again, day or night, they usually do. This is their home.

Twenty feet from the shoreline the snow became slushy. "Let's walk around the lake—it's too dangerous to cross," my friend said. The next morning, from our campsite high on a steep cliff, we could see open water on the lake just ahead of where our footprints had turned back.

As we rounded the lake, we passed a wooded hillside where I want my ashes to be spread. It's marked with a small pile of rocks and shaved sticks from a beaver dam. I thought about how most people prefer to be buried in nice clothes and how dead men often wear shoes.

When we found the place where we wanted to spend the night, we set up camp and ate. A small candle in the snow provided us with light. Our bedding consisted of a thin blue mat for insulation from the cold snow and a sleeping bag to protect us from the night air. We used a small shovel to dig and flatten an area in the snow where the mats and sleeping bags were placed. We had no tent or fire.

What was left of our bread, cheese, moose jerky, salami, cashews, and water was tucked inside our sleeping bags with our boots to keep them from freezing and close to the only source of warmth we had, our bodies. We were surrounded by fresh deer beds, splayed tracks, and droppings as we lay in the open under the stars.

Within an hour, the cold light of the moon appeared to our left over the treeline across the lake, where the dawn first appeared the next morning. But we were not alone that night.

Most people sit on their comfortable couches and watch TV on a winter night. We watched the stars. The twins, Castor and Pollux, were overhead, and the seven sisters, known as the Pleiades, were there too, as was the giant hunter, Orion. In Greek mythology, all seven sisters were once pursued by Orion. To save them, Zeus turned them all into doves and then stars.

According to Indian legend, the Pleiades were seven brothers who were awakened in the night by singing voices that made them dance. As

The author sleeping in the winter woods at night.
Photo courtesy of Steve Lukits.

Another one of our winter campsites. Patches of bare ice show where thin blue mats were placed for sleeping. Small dark hole in ice is where moose sausages were cooked the night before.
Photo courtesy of Steve Lukits.

they danced, the voices receded, drawing the brothers little by little into the sky, where the moon transformed them into a group of dancing stars. But one of the dancing brothers, upon hearing the weeping of his mother, looked backward and fell with such force that he was buried in the earth. As his mother mourned over him, a tiny sprout appeared that grew into a great tree that reached for the heavens. And so the pine was born the tallest of trees, the guide of the forest, and the watcher of the skies.

From my sleeping bag in the snow, I watched something happen that night that I have not seen before. It was something that those who named the stars and created their myths could never have imagined. High in the distance, the silent lights of a jet passed through the night sky leaving a vapour trail in its wake. It spread out behind the jet and looked like a thin ribbon, as long and white as the Milky Way.

Moved by the invisible winds high above us, the vapour trail drifted across the night sky and fell toward the horizon. It gradually faded while slowly descending beneath the shoulders of Orion, across his belt, and down the length of his sword toward his feet. I wondered what the first stargazers would have thought of ships that sail through the sky.

In the morning, we ate oatmeal and brown sugar mixed with water from melted snow. Later, we followed our footprints back through the woods and over the frozen lakes and swamps to the car. Along the way we saw other tracks that led to juniper bushes and cedar trees where rabbits and deer had eaten their breakfast. Near the end of our journey my friend said, "We're lucky to have all this."

Some people think I'm crazy or at least different because of "all this." Maybe I do spend too much time in the woods, especially at night. But one day it will probably all be gone except for the stars. On the drive home I remembered something else my friend said: "In the history of this part of the world, even if it never gets written, we have a place."

CHAPTER 2

If you sit in my workpen and look over my left shoulder, you'll see a picture of a lion.

I took that photo years ago in a petting zoo near Toronto. The lion paced quietly, desperately, and continuously back and forth along a worn path inside his cage.

At each turn, his great mane touched the bars as his gaze slipped through them, past me, to a wild and distant place.

He was, of course, insane.

WORLDS OF DISCOVERY

So much of our lives is consumed by simple, everyday routines, like travelling back and forth to work. Years ago I started walking between my home and the office for exercise. Step by step, it led to a new awareness inspired by the world I discovered around and inside me.

When I walk to work, I travel a short distance down Highway 15, through Barriefield Village, along the wooded shoreline of the Cataraqui River, across the three bridges of the La Salle Causeway, and past a sign that says: "Welcome to Kingston."

A year passed between the first time I saw the hoof tracks on the shoulder of Highway 15 and the living legs that made them. His shadowy figure was standing in the rain, grazing on clover beneath the limestone bell tower of St. Mark's Anglican Church. I've seen others like him, including a doe and two fawns. It was still dark that morning, but they were only a few feet away, standing as still as lawn ornaments, on the sidewalk in the middle of Barriefield Village.

Once, a red fox carrying the limp body of a black squirrel loped proudly across Highway 15, returning to its den. Paw prints in the snow led back to a tree behind an abandoned heritage house in Barriefield. The squirrel had died there minutes earlier, but he had been marked for death on a previous morning. That happened when the fox arrived early to watch him wake, leave his nest, and travel his regular route through the branches and down a certain familiar tree.

Great cunning and patience are needed by those who depend on fresh meat for survival. They watch for reassuring routines and wait for forgetful moments. When the fox returned and hid in the shadows near the foot of the tree, the squirrel's journey ended because he did not expect the unexpected.

Roadkill is also a grim and common sight along the highway. No crowds gather around the unlucky animal pedestrians. Only a few streetwise crows wait in the wings, ready to clean up after rush hour has passed.

The wooded shoreline along the Cataraqui River is a small but thriving wildlife sanctuary located within shouting distance of downtown Kingston. Snakes, partridge, and raccoons live out their secret lives here, and rabbits and groundhogs head for hidden holes at the sound of passing footsteps.

People with dogs and artists with easels visit this area. A woman with a poodle often stops and speaks to me. I reminded her of the other time our paths crossed, thirty years ago, when she was an art teacher at Riverdale Collegiate in Toronto and I was a student.

The weather takes a toll on the pedestrians crossing the La Salle Causeway. The waters and winds of the St. Lawrence and Cataraqui rivers and Lake Ontario converge here, pounding passersby with high gusts and spray from crested waves. On winter mornings, the wind chill turns your cheek and lowers your head. When the temperature hits minus 50°C, I stop on the lift-bridge, spitting slowly and deliberately onto the iron guardrail to hear it crackle before hitting and turning to ice on impact.

The only other year-round regular who crosses the causeway is "the running man." He is a jogging legend in Kingston, running all over town like a restless, wandering ghost. Alone together, we pass one another on the bridge each morning. We are not rivals but never speak, perhaps out of respect for the solitude we share. When the weather is extremely harsh, he doesn't run, and I am secretly pleased not to see him crossing the bridge.

When the good weather returns, anglers flock to the causeway, lowering hooks and lines into the hidden world beneath the bridge, where marauding pickerel hunt in packs like wolves.

In the distance, historic domes and spires stand above the downtown Kingston skyline as the Wolfe Island ferry glides by following its course. Sometimes while walking I do not feel the sun or wind or cold. I am alone, on an inner journey.

Walking anywhere, any time, is a simple pleasure, and best when done alone. Still, I've had some good companions who became friends through walking. Since Mary retired and Laura moved, I no longer leave little "notes" and sketches on those mornings when I find a fresh white canvas of snow. I still smile when I pass the place where they discovered my snow angel wearing a halo, a place where, minutes before, I awakened and rediscovered the child inside me.

CHAPTER 3

The mind is its own place, and in itself
Can make a heaven of hell, a hell of heaven

John Milton, Paradise Lost

THE SYMPHONY

A woman was telling me about a man who was invited to a fancy dinner party at a fine Kingston restaurant. She said he grew up as a farm boy and still lived a simple life in the small town of Westport, north of the city, the same place where she has lived all her life.

When she asked if he liked the dinner party, he replied: "Everyone was all dressed up, and I didn't have anything in common with the people sitting around me, and the food was nice to look at but it wasn't meat and potatoes." Then he said: "I'd rather be sitting on a rock in Lanark."

I remember laughing at the comment about the rock, probably because I thought he sounded like some kind of hillbilly. But his words stuck with me.

I don't know the man who spoke those words by name and am sure we have never met. I don't know what growing up on a farm is like, or how it feels living in a small town. I don't even know my way around Lanark County. But one day it suddenly occurred to me that I knew that rock.

The rock is your special place for whatever you like to do there. For the man from Lanark, the rock is Lanark and everything he does there, whether he's cutting hay or a hole in the ice to go fishing. Not everyone has a place like that, even though it can be any place at all, or more than one place, including a rock in Lanark. If you're lucky, your rock might be right in your own backyard, and if you're not, it may be

The author standing on his rock.
Photo courtesy of Steve Lukits.

far away, or close but hard to get to. But that means you enjoy getting to it almost as much as being there.

One of my favourite places really is a rock. I go there to sit, even though you can never just sit on a rock because you have to look and hear and think and feel while sitting there. My rock is a long way from the workpen where I sit most days surrounded by grey-panelled partitions and other workers in other workpens.

To get to the rock, I drive less than an hour from Kingston with my bike in the car. Then I ride my bike along an old railway bed before hiking through the woods. The rock is on a high bluff above the treetops overlooking a small lake.

The place where I sit is often stained white from the droppings of turkey vultures who also come there to perch. Nowadays there are few wild places that the noise of a car, boat, or tractor cannot reach. My lookout, though isolated, is no exception. I have been there often and occasionally heard human sounds.

I have given my own name to the place where I sit on the rock. I call it "The Symphony," even though there are times when the wilderness around, above, and below the rock does not make a sound or even move. Often when I come to visit, the wilderness just looks back

The author sitting on his rock.
Photo courtesy of Steve Lukits.

at me. I sit there inside it, surrounded by its beauty, dwarfed by its majesty, awed by its wildness.

No matter how many times I sit on that rock, the experience is always different, because the wilderness is not a painting or a recording or something that can be captured by a keystroke and reproduced on a piece of paper. The wilderness is a constantly changing living masterpiece.

I go to the rock to acknowledge the wilderness. I go there to let it know it is not alien to me. I even go there to show the wilderness that I have learned to love it. And sometimes it responds, after a long stillness. When the wind stirs, I can feel the wilderness breathe. And as it begins to move, there is a mute exchange between us like the silent communication between a mother and the child she carries in her womb. All while sitting on a rock. What I see and hear and feel there can't be measured, perfected, or given a value, because it is timeless, flawless, and priceless.

"I'd rather be sitting on a rock in Lanark." It took me a while to realize that I had heard words of wisdom.

CHAPTER 4

My office building is filled with people sitting in grey modular workpens connected by carpeted runways. One day, I noticed that the man sitting at the four-way intersection where you turn to walk to my cubicle had placed a small, smooth stone on top of a small cabinet in the outside corner of his office, where it could be easily seen by people passing. He told me it was a keepsake from his cottage on Wolf Lake near Westport.

I asked if I could put down a small stone of my own that I had found while hiking. Eventually I put down other totems that I had picked up in the woods, including a deer antler, beaver spike, turkey vulture feather, the discarded shed of a rat snake, and various animal skulls and bones.

A woman in my building whom I had just started to date came to my workpen for a visit. She said, "You sit near that weirdo with all the animal bones and body parts on his cabinet."

"Yes," I replied, "but those things are all mine."

QUEEN OF NIGHT

That night, the trees surrounding the shoreline of Hidden Lake looked like a giant army of crowned kings halted at the water's edge. They seemed to be patiently waiting for a glimpse of a secret and solitary queen who was about to pass before them.

We also were there to see her visit, perched high above the treetops on a smooth, rocky bluff overlooking the lake.

As darkness approached, the day sounds gradually faded, reluctantly giving way to the night sounds of the swamps and forest. A whippoorwill called its name, while lonely tree toads called for a mate.

The long, wide wings of a great blue heron creaked as it flew below us, searching for a place to hunt. In the near distance, a chorus of frogs sang out a warning, perhaps to the heron, telling him their wetland was "too deep, too deep," while the coarse voice of a lone bullfrog croaked, "Go round, go round." My friend asked: "When was the last time you looked down and saw a blue heron flying?"

Night in the wilderness does not descend from the sky, as it does in the city. It creeps out slowly from under the shadows and from beneath the dark places where it remains hidden, waiting patiently for the sunlight to pass.

As night inched forward around us, along with a soft and sudden glow that flickered and faded on the wings of busy fireflies, thoughts of another night slipped from my memory. We had been fishing, when someone on the boat pointed to their tiny lights, flashing in the blackness of the nearby shoreline. I knew he was poor as a boy because he liked to tell us how poor he once was.

He said: "I used to catch fireflies and keep them in a jar to use as a flashlight."

Then she appeared, slowly rising over the treetops directly across the lake, as if ascending from some black and fiery cauldron hidden deep beyond the darkness of the forest. Perfectly round, timeless, as red as grass is green, enthroned on high, the undisputed queen of the night sky had arrived.

"Shall we howl?" my friend asked. We only laughed. Perhaps we were too civilized to howl at something so powerful and beautiful. Where the moonlight touched the rippling water, both the light and lake came alive. A glimmering pathway of light danced across the lake from the shoreline beneath us, growing longer and glittering brighter as the moon rose higher.

The mosquitoes tested our resolve to stay and watch, though they themselves were pursued by snapping dragonflies, which in turn were pursued by hungry bats.

A single loon, black-hooded, white-breasted, and checker-backed, paddled into view, immersed in that beam of celestial light that penetrated deep into Hidden Lake. The loon's melancholy cry, unearthly yet unmistakable, only added to the perfect harmony of the silent spectacle before us. We spoke few words then, preferring the company of our private thoughts as the moon reached another place untouched by the light of day.

High above us, in a place once known as the heavens and now called space, a satellite sailed past, while the stars—silent worshippers, too—opened their eyes, one by one. Later, somewhere between space and our rock, out beyond our hearing, the blinking light of a large passenger plane flew by, heading eastward.

We finally left, but our adventure had not yet ended. We followed our moon shadows through the woods to our bicycles along the old railway bed. Boyish then, we pedalled a long way back to the car and drove home. By the time we arrived, the people in the plane were crossing the Atlantic Ocean. They were probably halfway to Europe.

CHAPTER 5

A friend of mine won a fishing derby in Brockville, Ontario. The prize was a million dollars.

We used to hunt and play hockey together. He liked hunting rabbits with a .22 rifle. I remember sitting in the dressing room staring at his hockey gloves and the rabbit pelt he had stitched over the palms when the leather wore through and exposed his hands.

The organizers of that fishing derby attached a tag to a largemouth bass with the name MAXAMILLION on it. If you caught the bass with the tag during a three-day contest, you won the million dollars.

He caught MAXAMILLION on the first morning.

One of the two men with him was amazed, "You just won a million dollars!"

But my friend just put the bass on a stringer over the side of the boat into the water. The three men kept fishing the rest of the day before returning to shore with the prize.

My friend liked winning the money, but he loved fishing more.

The causeway fishin' hole

A small piece of heaven, as great as all outdoors, has endured the test of time, and it's just a stone's throw from the heart of a city. It's the fishing hole located beside the La Salle Causeway that crosses the Cataraqui River. Kingston residents have "fished the bridge" since it was built in 1916 by the Department of Public Works Canada.

As the summer night spreads its wings and descends, anglers leave the city and flock to the bridge. The river is there, flowing and swirling beneath them. Fishermen are drawn by the dark, secret world hidden below. In it, night hunters have begun to feed.

There are pickerel, prized game fish also known as walleye. They have delicate, light-sensitive, bulging eyes that keep them near the cool, dark bottom during daylight hours.

There are smallmouth and largemouth bass, holding steady in the current with wavering fins. Both are compact, powerful fighters. When attacking, the largemouth bass can open its jaws wide enough to swallow a man's fist.

The greedy northern pike, a mainstay for fishermen at the bridge, also patrols these waters. It devours bait fish and baby ducks as it chases away other predators.

There are American eels, too, frightening, snakelike, and slimy. Their migration is even more remarkable than that of the salmon. They arrive here after a five-year journey from spawning grounds in the Sargasso Sea in the Bermuda Triangle. They stay another ten years before returning to their birthplace to begin another fascinating cycle of life.

Occasionally a sheepshead is caught, pale and post-nuclear looking. It has the body of a fish and a head like a sheep.

Farther offshore, near the old Woolen Mill, bullheads and carp forage for food. If fish have nightmares, the green monster that waits in ambush nearby is surely one of them. He is a master of murder and mayhem, with alligator-like jaws filled with sharp teeth, and a long, streamlined body built for quick, short bursts of speed. He is a natural cannibal who eats fish, snakes, birds, ducks, muskrats, and chipmunks. He can bend a barbed hook in his mouth and spit it out. He can weigh upwards of seventy pounds and live for thirty years. Occasionally, he even attacks people, especially those who like to dangle their feet in the water. This watery kingdom is ruled by a prince of darkness—the muskellunge.

A fishing friend told me he once saw a muskie take a black squirrel that was playing on a branch jutting over the water. The squirrel was gone in a heartbeat. The story of the squirrel brings to mind another sure sign of summer at the causeway. In a display of bravery or foolishness, young boys jump from the bridge into the cold water below. Like the squirrel who wandered out on a limb, they do it to feel the awe that dwells on the edge of fear.

Many anglers have pursued the muskie for years and have yet to catch one. But modern fishermen have learned to use technology to enhance their powers. Today, muskies are hunted by something they cannot see, smell, or feel. Lures that flash and thrash like struggling fish are used to trick the muskie. If one is caught, it is slowly exhausted in a spectacular tug of war that can take more than a half hour. Finally, it turns on its side and is swallowed up in the mouth of a net. Like other fish, many are set free, wiser and more wary.

Gulls also fish near the bridge. They hover above, drop to the water, and carry away small shad while other gulls try to steal their catch. The gull is a fascinating creature with knobby knees, webbed, clawed feet, and a demonic laugh. Most common are the ring-billed gulls, named for the dark ring at the end of their beaks. They're defiant, observant, opportunistic scavenger/hunters. On the waterfront, they also have the role of cleanup agents.

Upriver from the causeway, a channel curves around Belle Island. Its red-and-green buoys signal the way to the first lock of the Rideau Canal waterway, a half hour away by boat. The canal is a boater's paradise and engineering wonder, built during the 1830s through wilderness, rock, and swamp, under the supervision of Col. John By. The British government paid the bills. More than five hundred men died just from malaria during the five years it took to complete the canal.

The causeway fishing hole doesn't have the peace and serenity of a back lake. The steady buzz from speeding rubber tires crossing the narrow bridge of grated steel is a constant reminder of the surrounding city. Even the warning whistle of some distant train reaches the bridge. Despite the noise, the city still seems far away.

On the causeway, anglers relax as they chat and fish. Many wear ball caps and smoke cigarettes. Suddenly, there's a tug on a line. A rod bends and seems to come alive in the hands of a fisherman. As the line tightens, he doesn't hear the sound of the city or the voice that shouts: "Fish on!"

He hears only one thing: the soft, steady click from the drag of the reel, as something unseen pulls at the end of the line from the wilderness below.

CHAPTER 6

The first time I fell through the ice I was alone. As I broke through, I heard this terrible scream. As I struggled to get out of the freezing water, I remember wondering where it came from.

I realized later. It was my voice.

THE SPIRIT IN THE WOODS

We had hiked for about an hour when we emerged from the woods onto a frozen, snow-covered lake. High overhead, a long, unbroken V of Canada geese broke the silence as we began to cross.

The fury of winter had passed, so we each carried a long stick as a precaution against falling through the ice. Our shadows preceded us, one like a warrior holding a spear upright, the other like a tightrope walker balancing a pole sideways.

The author and his friend with their sticks.
Photo courtesy of Steve Lukits.

The remaining patches of wild woods and lakes north of Kingston still possess a powerful force drawing people back to nature. Trekking through the wilderness is both exercise and an escape from civilization.

Hiking through the woods is like visiting a ghost town. Nothing seems to move or be alive—until you stop, watch, and listen. Look at one thing long enough—a wildflower or a rock cut—and you begin to see clearly and think simply.

Look up. Watch the passing clouds and you will see time becoming time. Listen, and you might even hear a spirit moving through the woods. There will be a distant sound like rushing water, and then, as it approaches, rustling leaves and swaying branches. You will feel it wandering past, unseen, all around and high above you.

Or look down as you go. Tracks and animal droppings appear like words in a book. If you read them, they tell you what had passed before, how many, and when. Look closely. You can see where they fed and what they nibbled on. Follow along. You may find life hiding in unexpected places.

Be patient. A great and living work of art will gradually reveal itself. With each step, in any direction, a continuously changing masterpiece, with no beginning or end, will gradually appear.

While visiting the woods with a friend this winter, I witnessed a rare and unforgettable sight. Sunbeams created a dazzling spectrum of yellow, red, and orange lights diffracting through the ice crystals that covered the branches in the trees around us. It was a sight in broad daylight as bright and beautiful as Vincent Van Gogh's painting *Starry Night*.

But nature is deceiving. Songbirds that soothe our senses attack tiny creatures living on the forest floor. The wilderness is an uncaring and hostile place where mistakes are seldom tolerated. Forget "the early bird catches the worm" or "survival of the fittest." There are no rules here, only uncertainty. Life in this Garden of Eden is often a living hell.

I have always admired the bravery of animals that live in the wild. Fear and hunger are constant companions. Cold and darkness press in and down upon them as they struggle to survive while driven by the harsh logic of instinct.

The author listening to the wind.
Photo courtesy of Steve Lukits.

Wild animals do not have names like Thumper and Bambi, nor do they make friends or sing songs. Many are abandoned at an early age, without explanation, becoming elusive, secretive loners for most of their short lives. We fear death, thinking of it in quiet moments, pretending to understand it; but they fear dying, because almost all die violently. Some are swallowed whole and alive, others have their throats savaged or held shut as they slowly suffocate.

I was awestruck by the wilderness the first time I entered it. The wilderness links us to our beginning, to our original ancestors who climbed down from the trees, stood upright, and walked out silently and bravely over the open plains. There is a timeless spirit remaining in those woods and in the soul of every man and wild creature that ever drew a breath there.

I discovered why that spirit is in my soul the morning we crossed that frozen backwoods lake. The sticks were the key. We didn't carry them as weapons, but for protection, because we feared the wilderness. We are drawn to the wilderness not just because we are in awe of its beauty, but because we are afraid of its wildness.

We crossed the lake again on our way back home. The wind and snow had covered our old tracks, and it seemed as if we had never been there at all.

The shadow of the author against a rock cut in the woods.
Photo courtesy of Steve Lukits.

CHAPTER 7

As usual, it was dark when we left the tent that morning. There were three of us. We had walked a long way before stopping. Someone wanted a smoke. We were along a ridge overlooking the swamp where Francis would try and call a moose out.

It was still dark, but I saw it coming from a distance. I admired it just for a moment before I pointed and said to the others, "Look at that."

They both turned and looked but they did not see it.

Then Francis turned and asked me, "What is it? What are you looking at?"

"It's the dawn," I replied.

THE GREATER SIN

We entered the woods on foot near a small but uncrowded cemetery. In my coat pockets, I carried the same food as always: three oranges and two hard-boiled eggs.

Another season had just passed. It was early spring. I thought about a time to come when I wouldn't see another one. We stopped at the first swamp to look, listen, and receive. Farther along the trail, we stepped over a large rotting log, returning to the ground where it once lay buried as a tiny seed that later became the great tree it once was.

The long white backbone of a beaver had been carefully placed along the top of the log weeks earlier. My friend's daughter had found it. Now, whenever we passed this place, he would see the backbone and think of her. I would see the same bones, with scratches from tooth marks, and think of a fat beaver, far from his pond, gnawing instead of listening as death approached. I would see the living nightmare that haunted his dreams, and how it surprised him that day, and tore his throat open, spilling his blood, without emotion.

As we walked, I held out my bare hands, opening them and saying, "The air is liquid this morning, can you feel it?" He didn't answer. Later I said, "I want to eat an orange," which means, *let's stop*; which means, *let's talk*.

As I peeled the orange, he said, "Your oranges remind me of a painting by Turner that I saw in the Tate Gallery in London." He often talked about Turner's paintings, especially the one of Hannibal crossing the Alps with his army and elephants under a dark, stormy sky. Today, he described a painting of a sinking ship, and its cargo of oranges floating in the water around it. He spoke of a woman standing beside him in the gallery and how she turned and said to him, "Those oranges remind me of my life." Then, overcome by emotion, she wept.

As we continued hiking, I wondered about the awful truth she had seen in that painting and why it had moved her to tears, and how life is such a mystery.

When we rested again, I ate another orange. "You're littering the ground with those orange peels," he said. "They take too long to decay. I saw your rotting peels from previous weeks along the ridge we just came down." He told me, "those orange peels don't belong here," which I took to mean that I didn't belong.

He wanted me to pick them up and hide or bury them. I refused. But I knew if I left them, he would pick them up himself. To make it less awkward, I walked down to the lake and pretended to look at something in the water.

On our way out of the wilderness, it rained. We sat humped up under a stand of pines along the shoreline of Hidden Lake. I took out my last egg, and showed it to him in the palm of my open hand. "It's the perfect food," I said. Using the heel of my boot, I dug a hole and buried the shells. "That's good," he said. "You have redeemed yourself."

Now it was my turn. I reminded him of what had occurred that morning. Shortly after we entered the woods, we rounded a bend and surprised a beaver. It was ten yards away, dragging its big belly and flat tail across a worn game trail between two swamps.

Perhaps he can be forgiven for what he did because of his state of mind. It starts in the car, as we near our destination. He will raise his hand, and tell me to stop talking, because he's getting psyched and ready to enter the woods. When we first enter the wilderness, he walks fast because he's excited by the thought of becoming a part of it.

Maybe that's why he decided to chase the beaver that morning, all the way to its pond. The beaver thought it was running the race between fear and hunger like the rabbit and the fox, and the squirrel and the fisher.

The beaver usually runs this race against a wolf or coyote. As the beaver cuts down more and more trees around its pond, it must travel farther and farther to the next tree. It's your life that kills you in the end, and it's no different for the beaver. One day a wolf will come over a ridge and spot the beaver far from the safety of its pond. That's when the beaver and wolf will race.

At one point my friend got so close to the beaver I thought it would turn on him and leave a big hole in his leg, like the kind I've heard they leave in the throats of wolves and coyotes and sometimes dogs. He even yelled or growled something at the beaver. "Who made that sound, you or the beaver?" I asked.

It was obvious he intended no harm, but the beaver didn't know that. It was afraid, which means it had to fight its attacker or flee to the safety of its pond, which means the beaver felt it was caught in a moment of life or death.

I told my hiking partner that if I had sinned by leaving orange peels on the ground, he had committed an even greater sin. "You scared the hell out of that beaver," I said. "Just for your own pleasure."

CHAPTER 8

He began to accompany his mother on the meat-trail, and he saw much of the killing of meat and began to play his part in it. And in his own dim way he learned the law of meat. There were two kinds of life—his own kind and the other kind. His own kind included his mother and himself. The other kind included all live things that moved. But the other kind was divided. One portion was what his own kind killed and ate. This portion was composed of the non-killers and the small killers. The other portion killed and ate his own kind, or was killed and eaten by his own kind. And out of this classification arose the law. The aim of life was meat. Life itself was meat. Life lived on life. There were the eaters and the eaten. The law was: EAT OR BE EATEN. He did not formulate the law in clear, set terms and moralize about it. He did not even think the law. He merely lived the law without thinking about it at all.

From White Fang *by Jack London*

"C'EST LA CUISINE SAUVAGE"

Carrying the meat is my responsibility. I carry it for miles and hours and always on my back.

We routinely stop to make a fire to cook and eat the meat about the same time in the woods north of Kingston.

One morning three of us were hiking. It was an hour before dawn and too early for trail talk. But I stopped anyway to say something to the man behind me. I spoke softly as men often do in the dark.

"You've been coming here with us for a couple of years now. Would you like to take a turn carrying the meat?" I asked.

"I'd consider it an honour," he replied.

As I passed him the knapsack, I said, "The meat will taste better for you today."

We stopped at about nine a.m. to eat on a granite ridge along the shoreline of a place we have named Lookout Swamp because we go there often to sit and look. When we agree on a spot to stop, we immediately prepare the fire.

We pick up rocks and put them in place to contain and protect the hearth. We gather thin strips of birch bark, dry twigs, and dead branches before starting the fire with a wooden match. The cook places his homemade stainless steel wire grill across the rocks when the wood coals are glowing.

That's when I take the venison from the knapsack. Table talk goes across and around the fire as the meat cooks over it. Pieces of meat that are too small for the grill are eaten raw.

Someone at the fire points to the meat and says, "It still has bits of white hair on it."

I just laugh and say, "You can't get quality like that from town meat, not even at a butcher shop."

I asked the man who carried the meat if it felt heavy on his back.

He replied, "Carrying the meat lifted my spirit. It lightened my load."

"That's right," I said. "I know how it feels."

Later as we sat and ate our wild meat he said something that must have come from someplace memorable in his past. He did not speak in English. He spoke in fluent French. While speaking, he made a wide sweeping motion with his hand towards the rocks, trees, brush, and swamp beside the fire.

He said, "*C'est la cuisine sauvage.*"

His words, which translate to, "*It's the savage kitchen,*" were the right words for capturing the moment and our place in the woods.

When the wild meat is on the grill, the cook turns it with his bare fingers—which he often burns. After cooking, he places the meat on a flat rock and cuts it into pieces with a Swiss Army knife. We eat from the rock with our hands. In winter it's often so cold that the fire provides little warmth unless you remove your gloves and put your hands close to the flames. But the hot meat warms us from the inside. Later, like coyotes at a kill site, we move on when the venison is gone.

The meat has a long journey before reaching our fire and entering our woods. I am the only hunter at our fire. I often tell the story of how the deer or moose that we are about to eat became wild meat. I tell where and how it died.

The author and his friend cooking wild meat in the woods.
Photo courtesy of Steve Lukits.

I often helped gut and drag it to a road, or hoist it up a meat pole, or skin it, or load and deliver it to a slaughterhouse, and return to pick it up and bring it home, and put it in my freezer, and thaw it piece by piece, and marinate it for days, before finally putting it in my knapsack to carry back to the woods.

For me, wild meat and especially venison is big medicine. Few animals are as wild as a woodland deer. They are alert and elusive and tough. They are not tame and docile and fat like domestic animals. They spend much of their lives avoiding death and danger. And unlike most wild animals, they sleep outside day and night all winter long with no nest or cave or hole to crawl into for protection.

When I eat deer meat I believe that I eat the essence of what made that deer strong and healthy and wild and pure. The physical and mental vigour of that animal becomes part of me.

Some people say wild meat is good for your sex life. A white-tailed buck would mate any time of the year if a doe would let him. But he must wait for a few frantic weeks in the fall when does are in heat and become receptive to his urges. That means white-tailed deer are in rut during hunting season. During that time, a buck's neck swells as hormones rage inside with anticipation. Sometimes he finds no relief, because he is killed. Then his meat becomes my flesh and his blood flows in my veins.

There are many rituals *dans la cuisine sauvage,* from wood gathering to fire starting to cooking and even to covering the hearth and leaving the woods as we found them. We have one ritual you seldom see at any table. It honours the hunter as the provider of the feast. In the savage kitchen, he is given the first piece of wild meat to eat.

CHAPTER 9

They have cradled you in custom,
they have primed you with their preaching,
They have soaked you in convention through and
through;
They have put you in a showcase; you're a credit to their
teaching —
But can't you hear the Wild?—it's calling you.

From Call of the Wild *by Robert Service*

CALL OF THE WILD

The name on the tires of the four-wheel-drive SUV parked along the curb on Princess Street stopped me in my tracks.

They were Firestone tires. But they also had a special name like the SUV. It was stamped in large, white, block letters on the black rubber sidewalls. They were WILDERNESS AT (All Terrain) tires and the SUV was an EXPLORER.

As I walked away, I began to think that there was something wrong with Sport Utility Vehicles and people who drive them.

Television commercials show people driving SUVs over rugged mountains, across flooded creeks, and through back woods. But I've yet to see an SUV out exploring the wilderness or parallel parking between two trees in a forest like one does in another SUV commercial.

In reality, most SUVs never venture off paved roads in cities and towns except while driving on the highways connecting them. In this part of the world, SUV country is south of the 401. And people who drive fully equipped SUVs don't worry about getting lost. If they're out exploring a new subdivision or on an expedition to a far-off shopping mall, they'll always be prepared in case they get turned around. By pressing a button on their dashboard, a computerized navigational system will guide them to the next traffic light or major intersection.

I can't remember seeing a Sport Utility Vehicle in a sport utility place like a hunting camp or construction site. I've never seen a Sport Utility Vehicle involved in a sport utility activity like hauling a load of wood or taking garbage to the dump. Most of the SUVs that I've seen look like they just left a car wash. My sport utility mountain bike has more dirt and mud on it than many of the SUVs driving around Kingston.

I've seen a lot of people using Sport Utility Vehicles to pick up their morning coffee at drive-thrus and to transport groceries home at night. I've never driven or even been inside an SUV, but I've heard that they have safe and sturdy cup holders to prevent dangerous spills. And you can store plenty of plastic grocery bags in the rear cargo space of an SUV without having to bend over and risk hurting your back like you would while loading the trunk of a car.

People in the auto industry had the insight to realize that potential SUV customers have something missing in their lives. They filled that void and their pockets by making buyers believe that the SUV is more than just a vehicle. They designed and marketed their product to make consumers think that the SUV also provides you with a brand-new sport utility image.

SUVs are deliberately given names like Avalanche, Escape, Expedition, Highlander, Land Rover, Navigator, Pathfinder, Trailblazer, and Yukon because the sport utility people who buy them want other people to think that they are "out there" having exciting adventures in wild places because they drive SUVs.

No one can connect with the great outdoors by looking through the tinted glass windows of an SUV that can weigh up to 5,000 pounds and cost up to 70,000 dollars. The true wilderness is no place for any kind of motorized vehicle. Even the sound of an engine is an intrusion inside the wild.

Buying an SUV is admitting that you've given up trying to connect with nature. It's like saying that you're too soft or old or lazy to get "out there" because you would rather feel safe and be secure inside a big, spacious machine with luxury leather seats, sturdy cup holders, a DVD entertainment system, 3-D navigation, and all-terrain tires with the word WILDERNESS written on them.

On Earth Day during the 2004 election race in the U.S., presidential hopeful John Kerry was asked about the Chevy Suburban at his Idaho home. He replied. "I don't own an SUV. My family does." It turns out his wife and kids have three SUVs between them.

It's important to ask why Kerry avoided answering the question and telling the truth. Probably because he wants to be president of the United States of America. He obviously felt that distancing himself from SUVs would help him achieve that goal. His answer clearly shows that owning a SUV is still not politically correct. The stigma remains that SUVs are big, expensive gas-guzzlers that are harmful to the environment.

But SUV owners aren't breaking any laws or hurting anyone in particular. Everyone who drives a car is polluting and poisoning the planet to some extent. Many families have two small or mid-sized cars, which is probably worse on the environment than owning one SUV or pickup truck.

People have the right to own any type and drive any number of vehicles that they can afford. If driving an SUV makes someone happy, who am I to say don't drive one? The truth is that there's nothing wrong with SUVs and the people who drive them. I don't even have a problem with the corporations who make them.

But I object to the way corporations *market* SUVs because they are using the wilderness to sell a product. If all SUV owners drove over mountaintops, across creek beds, and through woodlands there would be no wilderness left to enjoy. Even though corporations know SUVs can't reach those places, they show disrespect for the wilderness by making people think they can sell something for profit even if it is just an illusion.

Smart marketers know that most people have lost touch with the wilderness. But they also realize that because we all come from the wilderness, we all still feel some attachment to it—like the bond that remains between a mother and the grown child she once nourished inside her womb.

Marketers understand the power of that bond. The exploitation of that link to our past is portrayed in another TV commercial showing four men sitting inside an SUV parked in the middle of a dangerous-looking suspension bridge made of wood and rope. As the bridge and SUV begin swaying gently over the steep mountain gorge below, the four men smile and take out their pillows. Then they lie back and close their eyes to have a nap and sweet dreams like babies being rocked to sleep in the cradle by a loving mother.

I can't tell you what babies dream about in their cradles. But I think I know what was in the dreams of those four men in the wilderness. They were dreaming about what they once were and where they came from.

CHAPTER 10

Local people who write columns for newspapers are treasures for the paper and its readers. The Whig-Standard *is among Canada's richest newspapers. The people in the picture show why.*

Newspaper photo showing about thirty *Whig-Standard* local columnists gathered at the newspaper on Monday for a double celebration.
Photo courtesy of Jack Chiang.

About thirty of The Whig*'s columnists, who represent hundreds of other local people we welcome to write columns for us every year, attended a double celebration at the newspaper on Monday. They gathered at our Woolen Mill offices for the book launch of Christine Overall's* Thinking Like a Woman.

The newspaper also invited other Whig *columnists who were able to attend. We wanted to celebrate their rich contribution to the newspaper.*

Readers will recognize some familiar faces. The man standing with the deer antler is L.W. Oakley, who has sparked controversy and outrage with his columns about local hunting camps—but he has also written about opera.

MOST POWERFUL SYMBOL OF WILDERNESS

While wandering on weekends so often over the years through the woods, I had only once found a deer antler lying on the ground. Although male white-tailed deer shed their antlers each winter, it's extremely rare to find one. They are covered by blowing leaves and falling snow, or gnawed on and eaten by porcupines, squirrels, chipmunks, and mice for their high calcium content.

On this day in early spring, we were moving through the woods as we always have, the only way you should—in single file, like animals, for safety. We were on high ground with large oak trees separated by small open meadows. It was surrounded by swamp on two sides and steep rocky edges on another. It was an area where we had never been before. Suddenly I felt that something unusual was about to happen. My feeling was so strong that I immediately stopped to look around. When the man behind me caught up, I turned and said, "Something is going to happen here."

He looked at me and said, "Really?"

He walked ahead and within a few minutes he pointed and shouted, "Look, an antler!"

We returned to that same area on our next four hikes and found five more antlers. No two antlers are exactly the same. But all of the antlers we found were distinctly different and probably came from six different deer.

Deer usually drop or shed their antlers within a day of each other, which means two antlers from the same deer can be located miles apart when they hit the ground.

People are surprised to hear that bucks grow and shed new antlers each year. The antler cycle usually starts in June and ends the following January. Antlers should not be confused with horns, which are made of protein called keratin and grow continuously from the heads of animals like bison and bighorn sheep. Antlers are bones that grow outside the body and appear only on males, with the exception of caribou.

I started asking people who spend time in the woods or who have hunted all their lives how many antlers they have found over the years. A typical answer was that they had never found an antler or that they had only found one.

The antler has three main roles in the life of whitetail deer, and using antlers as weapons for defence against predators is not one of them. If that were the case, both sexes would have antlers and they would not be shed every winter when they're needed most.

Antlers are used to establish dominance. In the fall when the days grow colder, the amount of sunlight passing through the eye of a deer decreases, causing testosterone levels to increase. Bucks instinctively begin to spar by using their antlers to push each other to determine who is stronger and who shall win the right to mate.

Antlers are also used to create signposts. During the rut, the rough base of the antler is used to strip bark from trees and create a rub, which is an invitation to receptive females and a warning to rival males.

Thirdly, the size and shape and thickness of antlers attract does, since a big rack indicates good health and fitness and vigour.

As we continued returning to that same place in the woods, we found numerous well-worn runways and rubs, including three rubs on three separate trees inches apart. We also began to see a lot of deer. They obviously felt comfortable in these surroundings due to the good food source and because they could easily detect approaching danger at a distance. But if we found this place, predators had to. The deer would still have to outrun or outlast the pursuit and hunger of coyotes. We soon found a number of kill sites in the area.

Antlers also have a strong attraction to people, especially hunters, who consider them trophies. An Alberta man recently sold the world-record mule deer antlers for $171,000 US. The prize antlers, which are famous in hunting circles, had been in his family since his father shot the buck in 1926.

Throughout time, antlers have been used as weapons and tools and in religious worship. Native people create art by carving antlers into the shapes of other animals. Antlers have also been used as medicine.

The antler is so powerful that it can even be used against deer to kill them. Hunters have learned to rattle two antlers together to turn the tables on deer and make them hunt the hunter. During the rut, smashing and rattling two antlers together with your hands can make a big buck obsessed with mating think that two other male deer are fighting over a doe in his territory. He will sometimes respond by charging through the woods directly toward the source of the sound.

The wilderness has always been my inspiration for writing. It is a source of power and strength for me. It has taught me patience and humility. It has given me insight into life and death. I have always known but never acknowledged that fact with written words. But I did try to show the readers of *The Kingston Whig-Standard* newspaper where my inspiration to write comes from on May 12, 2001. I showed it in a photograph, which appeared in the Whig-Standard that day.

The picture was taken at a formal gathering of about thirty writers who provide material for the *Whig*. All the writers and *Whig* editorial staff gathered for a group photo by *Whig* photographer Jack Chiang.

Just before he was ready to take our picture, Jack smiled and said, "Say cheese."

At that moment I lifted my arm to my chest and held up the most powerful symbol of wilderness.

CHAPTER 11

As a boy, I always liked TV programs about wild animals and nature like Mutual of Omaha's Wild Kingdom. *My father and I watched them together.*

When I was older, I occasionally left Toronto on business. While driving and travelling alone, I would look at the trees that lined what I thought was the edge of the wilderness. I wondered what it was like beyond the trees. I would think about what I had seen on TV and imagine what it was like to live inside the wilderness.

I didn't realize it then, but I had no idea what was beyond that treeline.

What happens when the wilderness responds

There were two bears and two men this time. They came together suddenly, but not accidentally, somewhere inside the disappearing wilderness north of Kingston.

One bear emerged from a swamp. The other bear was named Old Ben. It emerged from a book written by the great American writer William Faulkner.

I was one of the two men the evening it happened. We entered the wilderness, as we so often did, by riding our mountain bikes along an abandoned railway line. We stopped and watched snapping turtles digging holes and laying eggs in the soft warm earth beside the railway bed, where marauding raccoons would unearth and eat them before the young turtles hatched.

We hid the bikes before hiking to an isolated lake surrounded only by trees and rock and open sky. We swam in the lake as we always did, the best way you can, naked and without towels for drying.

The author swimming naked at Hidden Lake.

Standing beside the lake after our swim, we watched spectacular aerial hunters pursuing prey as they had 300 million years ago—100 million years before there were even dinosaurs. In the few feet of space between the surface of the lake and the branches of the trees immediately above our heads, damselflies and dragonflies were catching and eating deer flies and mosquitoes in mid-air.

Two dragonflies caught our attention. They were mating. They continued flying and copulating even as the tip of the male's long, slender, and now-curved abdomen entered her body.

Eventually, they landed together on the surface of the water, unaware of the world beneath, a place more deadly than the one above.

A small yellow perch also watched the dragonflies. It rose slowly from the warm shallow weed beds below, releasing air from its bladder as it did. Once within range, the fish exploded upon the dragonflies, pulling them down beneath the surface. But it did not know there were two dragonflies, and as the perch swallowed the female, the male escaped and managed to get one wing out of the water and into the air before the perch struck again. The entire drama ended in seconds. By then, even the ripples that remained behind had almost disappeared.

I carried food in a knapsack that also held a book with Faulkner's story called "The Bear." After swimming and eating, we read aloud from that book, which is something we had never done before while sitting in the dying sunlight on the still-warm rock high above the trees around the lake.

I read first. As I did, we entered the imagination of William Faulkner and the November woods of the American South. The story is about a once-invincible and savage bear, Old Ben, who never actually existed but who ruled over those woods; and the untamed men and dogs who never really lived but who hunted and killed the bear in Faulkner's imagined Yoknapatawpha County in the state of Mississippi.

We saw our bear in a swamp. It was swimming alone, moving silently through the dark, still water across the surface of the swamp. We could not see its red eyes or the small white patch on its chest, but when it rose up from the swamp and shook water from its thick black fur, starting from its head as a wolf would, we could see its powerful clawed limbs and its enormous shapeless body.

The bear never looked at us. As it moved away, its body seemed to melt back into the wilderness the way a wet patch of spring snow melts back into the warm earth. Because we had been in those woods so often and had only ever seen one other bear, I felt something significant, even mystical, had happened. Though I had seen and been part of it, I did not understand it.

When the bear disappeared, I said: "It was the book. We never brought a book here before, and we brought it to read about that bear, the one Faulkner wrote about and made famous, the one that represents the vanishing wilderness."

What I should have said was: "That bear let us see it, or maybe something else did, something that has been here all along, something that looks back when we come here to look, something that never leaves when we do, something that finally acknowledged our presence, something that shows itself only to those who are worthy and humble enough."

But I didn't say all that. Instead, I pointed toward the swamp where the bear had been and said: "That's what happens when the wilderness responds."

CHAPTER 12

I hike a lot. Almost every Saturday morning. I go with the same friend to the same wilderness north of Kingston. We leave early and are usually in the woods before the dawn. It was six years before we saw another person hiking.

Each time is different. Each time unique. The weather and seasons keep changing. The wildlife is more or less active depending on the time of day and year. The look, smell, sound, and feel of the woods changes almost with each step or turn of the head. But sometimes something really unusual happens.

One winter, we were finishing our hike. We were about twenty minutes from the edge of the wilderness when I spotted something coming through the woods about fifty yards away. My instinct was to duck down low to the ground and make myself small and hard to detect. I signalled with my hands to my friend to get down and be quiet. A man was coming through the woods. He had a beard and wore a toque and plaid jacket. There was a knapsack on his back.

He passed within feet of us but he never knew we were there. We crouched as he passed and remained silent until he disappeared.

We had not acted like men. We had behaved like animals.

I AM A PLACE THAT YOU MAY NEVER KNOW

I am birds that sing and the promise of spring. I am morning mist on marshes, a smiling sun at noon, the first star awake, and the cry of a loon. I am turning leaves that fall and rutting moose that call. I am the long winter that comes early and stays late.

I am the light in dark at the break of day and the dark in light that first appears as grey. I am protruding rock ridges that are the bones of the earth and the streams and valleys they lie beside. I am a place where lakes reflect the world they see around them. And I am the ice that seals their eyelids shut in winter. I am a place where life depends on listening and I am always listening and watching, too. I am a place where the wind is a constant visitor and trusted friend. I am a place where ears and noses detect the sound and scent of danger long before alert and wandering eyes find it.

I am the white patch on the throat of a white-tailed deer and the dark shadow moving silently across the ground behind it without snapping a twig or bending a blade of grass. I am hollow trees and black stumps and the black bear who rules over this place that is a place without rules.

I am the high wide swaying rack of a long-legged bull moose and the yellow eyes of a pack of timber wolves watching the tip of its antler dip lower than it should when its limp right hoof presses down on the soft grey moss. The wolves will come closer only if the moose tries to rest or eat and they will let it do neither now. I am a place where killing time has a different meaning. I am a place with no beginning or end, and for some, no way out.

I am a place where little has changed. I am the yellow beak of the blue heron, a living dinosaur and deadly impaler, who stands motionless and alone like a phantom laced in sunlight or veiled in shadow waiting patiently for some unwary creature to wander too close before spearing it.

I am the teeth and claws of the secretive fisher who uses its cunning to kill porcupines and its speed and agility to pursue squirrels up and through the trees.

I am tracks in the snow and the naked feet that keep the game trails worn. I am feathered wings that follow a path made in the mind across the trackless sky. I am the fur-bearing animal, the trapper's line and sudden death without overtime. And I am the hunting camp where men live life a different way, heading for swamps before first light and talking across open fires beneath the stars at night.

I am a place filled with fatherless children where childhood ends early if it ever begins at all. I am a place where nature is the mother of all things. I am the harsh logic called instinct, which is the only gift nature provides her children to guide them on their journey.

I am a place that must rot to remain unspoiled. I am a place where nothing really dies. I am a place where the flesh of one animal becomes the flesh of another until it returns to the ground where rainfall and sunlight make it rise up again to be nibbled at and fed on during a never-ending cycle of life. I am a place where everything is connected and all things depend on each other for survival. I am a place where life seems simple, which means it's complicated.

I am the Canadian beaver, the dams it makes and swamps it creates. I am water bugs scurrying across the surface of those swamps. And I am the world beneath the surface, which is even more dangerous than the one above because it is a place where all things live and die in silence.

I am bullfrogs and black snakes and snapping turtles that hunt and are hunted along its shorelines. I am the scented cedars and white pines and hard maples beyond the swamps and the wind that makes them bend and bow and creak and moan. And I am the sound of axes and saws gnawing away at the edges of this place.

I am a place that was once like the place where you live; but that was a long time ago. I am a place with a timeless spirit where light and dark, water and wind, rocks and trees, and all the animals that live and die beneath its sky can touch your soul. I am a place that will challenge and humble and teach those who enter it. I am a place that we are drawn to and fear, for the same reason.

I am the wilderness.

ABOUT THE
AUTHOR

Larry Oakley was born and raised in downtown Toronto and graduated from Riverdale Collegiate and Ryerson University. He moved to Kingston in 1977 and became a professional accountant (CMA).

He is a registered member of the Ontario Metis Aboriginal Association and has been freelance writing as a hobby for over ten years.

He goes deer hunting for two weeks every November.

His next book, *Outside the Wild,* will be released in 2008.